Date Due

THE REDISCOVERY OF JONES

THE REDISCOVERY OF JONES

Studies in the Obvious

BY

SIMEON STRUNSKY

"For it was the glory and charm of these primitive peoples that they had Folkways and Lores; whereas the American people had only customs and manners."

Essay Index Reprint Series

BOOKS FOR LIBRARIES PRESS, INC.

FREEPORT, NEW YORK

81147
First published 1931
Reprinted 1967

CONTENTS

THE REDISCOVERY OF JONES

I

THE REDISCOVERY OF JONES

In the new mood which is reported to have come over the spirit of America toward the end of the 1920's, and in the new books that should reflect this new temper, what is likely to happen to Jones? He is the person who figures so prominently in the returns of the United States Census. He is, in the majority, white. He is, in the majority, of native white parentage. He is male. He is thirty-eight years old. He is married. He is an advertising solicitor. He lives at 1437 West Eleventh Street. In numbers he is, together with his wife and children, his parents and cousins, several scores of millions. But in the solid books dealing with the American people and American civilization he was quite generally overlooked in the now elapsed 1920's. Will it be different in the current 1930's?

To raise the question of Jones on the threshold of a new age is normal procedure for us plain folk. We are not like the professional prophets. They, when confronted with the dawn of a new age, insist on addressing to it a comprehensive, a universal Whither? They, when informed that with the approach of the 1930's the spiritual climate of the United States entered upon a noticeable change, — from negation to affirmation; from disillusion to a renewed faith; from the satirical approach to the sympathetic approach; from destructive analysis to constructive synthesis, — the professional augurs, upon hearing of such things, immediately began to ask questions about American Civilization in the 1930's and American Destiny in the 1930's, with separate chapters on the Thirties and Religion, the Thirties and the Machine, the Thirties and Woman, the Thirties and children, music, art, architecture, football, labor, radio, aviation, armaments, the League of Nations; in other words, the Thirties and Everything.

We plain amateurs are content with much less than the cosmic vision. For us the advent of a new age means sitting down and looking, so to speak, into the wood fire of the imagination, and wondering what the times will bring, not to Civilization or to Humanity, but to our own particular little interest, or hobby, or foible. In the present instance it is Jones. What will an age of affirmative, sympathetic, constructive synthesis do to promote our knowledge and understanding of Jones, who is white, thirty-eight, married, and so forth? After all, it is Jones who in the 1930's will attend or not attend the churches in whose future there is so much interest. He is the man who will live in the architecture of the thirties, shout at the football games, develop the aviation, pay for the music and the radio, and be seriously affected by the armaments. What will happen to him in the new books of the new decade?

Well, to ask the question is to answer it. If the new books reflecting the new thought of the next ten years in America are to be affirmative, if they are to be sympathetic, if they are to strive for synthesis instead of riot, then it ought to be a pretty good time for Jones. The years immediately ahead of us are bound to witness the rediscovery of the ordinary American man in his normal recognizable aspects — him and his wife, and his young, and his newspapers, and his automobiles, and his political parties and opinions, and his industries and recreations. People in the new books ahead of us may be expected to resemble one's actual familiar neighbors — the familiar groups, the familiar individuals, the familiar behavior that so often find themselves submerged.

Submerged by what? Chiefly, one would say, by the formulas, and the slogans, and the doctrines. Take a man or group of men, launch a formula about them, ride that formula-hobby hard enough, and you will soon be out of sight of that man or group of men or the human race, careering at your own sweet will through a universe entirely of your own making. It is a familiar experience. An age will set out to smash the established idols, and it will end up with a fine new collection of images of its own. A generation proclaims war to the knife upon sham, and it develops in the course of hostilities its own equipment of hollow loyalties, slogans, stencils. A decade goes forth resolutely to face the facts, at the cost of no matter what heartbreak, and it succeeds in accumulating many more broken facts than broken hearts. A generation will resolve to pierce beneath the surface of life to the inner, essential meaning of things; and sure enough it will succeed in getting beneath the surface, but only to get beyond its depth in the inner meaning of things; having forgotten in the process how much of the meaning of life lies on the surface of life, and is to be apprehended by the innocent eye and the simple heart.

Creative Statistics

But in speaking of Jones and what the books of the past decade did to him, and what the books of the next ten years are likely to do to him, it is necessary to distinguish between books and books.

The problem of Jones concerns only the "serious" books.

The novelist may do what he likes with Jones, because he is dealing with an individual Jones. You protest that you don't find Jones in the new novel true to life, and the author looks up and says, "You don't recognize Jones? Well, I should hope not. This is n't Jones, but a satire on Jones written for the purpose of waking him up." And the creative biographer will say, "You don't recognize in my portrait the Edgar Allan Walt Waldo Jones whom you studied in your high-school American Literature? Of course you don't. This is n't E. A. W. W. Jones — it is a spiritual photograph of six of his selected sonnets." And creative biographer number 2 says, "Naturally you find it hard to identify in my new book the George Thomas Andrew Abraham Jones about whom you studied in your school history. You see, what I have done is to strip the man naked, reduce him to elemental planes, and pass him through the flame of my own temperament." It is the only way in which you may start out with Jones who lives at 1437 West Eleventh Street and sells life insurance, and end up by penetrating to the real, essential, naked Jones who lives in a Kafir kraal and worships strange fears and fetishes.

The argument is a sound one. Any individual

Jones in Marietta, Ohio, may become, in respect to character, manners, morals, language, clothes, and dietary habits, whatever the genius of his creator is able to make him. If you have the necessary ability you may do to Jones of Ohio what Dickens did to Micawber or Mark Twain to Huck Finn. You may write a book about a man named Jones who lives in Hartford and whose native language is Turkish: he was born in Angora of American missionary parents. You may have a man named Jones in Schenectady living in an igloo: he is the survivor of an Arctic expedition and slightly touched in the head. You may have a Jones in Mount Vernon, New York, who goes about naked: he is the leader of a sun cult and does his promenading in the privacy of his own grounds. The novelists and poets can do anything they please with Jones.

It is quite another matter with the men who write books on economics, social science, politics, democracies, schools, elections, newspapers, movies, automobiles, factories, and families. The man who deals with Jones in the mass, with Jones of the United States Census, cannot invoke the rights of his own vision and his own temperament. He is limited in his findings by certain basic data which no amount of creative inspiration can transcend. No amount of genius and no intensity of purpose will justify you in saying that the native language of the people of Hartford is Turkish, or that the dominant style of domestic architecture in Schenectady is the igloo, or that the 8.45 from Mount Vernon is crowded by commuters wearing just nothing. The latest finding of the New Physics asserts that truth is only statistical. There is no telling beforehand how one electron will behave. But one can foretell with certainty how ten billion electrons will behave. With respect to any one atom you may be a creative artist. With respect to the community of atoms you must stick to the statistical facts.

The heart warms as one peers into the future and sees the serious authors engaged in sticking to the facts about Jones, the Crowd Man. If the subject is Jones and the American press, the author will take a good deal of pains to ascertain what an American newspaper really contains. If the subject is Jones and his political parties, the author will not generalize from the New Psychology or from the dogmas of the British Labor Party, but will concentrate on the figures for the Presidential election of 1920, of 1924, of 1928, and the Congressional elections of 1930. The mind looks down the long vista of years, perhaps as far as the year 1940 and the next change in intellectual climate, and sees the serious authors keeping their eye on the ball, — that is to say, on

Jones,—and not on the grand stand where blossom the formulas, the slogans, the fashions, and the epigrams. The imagination sees Jones of Hartford receiving in the next decade the same sympathetic consideration that students of civilization in the preceding decade brought to the study of the Protochukchi Confederation.

The Primitives

The Protochukchis are a private discovery of the present writer. They are a group of tribes, probably of Bushman stock, occupying the wooded country about the headwaters of the Mulligatawney River in Central Patagonia. Under different names they were not unknown to the earlier anthropologists, but their enormous vogue dates only from the Armistice. Since that time everything has been said about the Protochukchis that possibly could be said, and with a richness of sympathy and understanding such as one vainly looks for in contemporary observations on the inhabitants of Evanston, Illinois.

Take, for example, the annual delousing festival of the Protochukchi Confederation. This enormously significant folk-muster, as it has been called, falls at the time of the spring equinox. Professor Dunkler (my own discovery) speaks of it as the focal point of the Protochukchi communal life.

H. J. Bias (my own discovery) refers to it as the nucleus around which cluster the warmest group loyalties and the tenderest personal memories. In describing this picturesque and poignant ritual, the student of civilization in the 1920's was as likely as not to say: — ". . . a vitalized Protochukchi group-consciousness integrated around the annual reënactment of vernal capillary evacuation." Or something of the sort.

On the other hand, well into the early months of the year 1929, when speaking of the average middle-class resident of Indianapolis, with his bathtub, his vacuum cleaner, his parquet floors, his cross ventilation, his high schools, his riding clubs, and his symphony orchestra, it was a not uncommon practice among students of American civilization to refer to him as "the Babbitt in his warren."

The idea, of course, is easily grasped. The Protochukchis dwell in caves dug out of the muddy banks of the Mulligatawney River, two hundred inhabitants to a cave. The resultant living conditions, sanitary, ethical, and æsthetic, impressed the modern observer as being essentially and lovably human. But the average American family, four people to the five-room apartment, suggested to the dispassionate eye of the observer nothing so much as a vermin swarm. Indeed, that elegant and impressive phrase about the Babbitt and his warren compels the imagination to go further. It evokes the Protochukchi mother in her cave as giving birth to her young, whereas the American mother apparently added to the population of the United States by littering. To such heights of sympathetic identification on the one hand (Protochukchi), and cool detachment on the other (Syracuse, New York), did the study of civilization attain in the United States in the decade after 1920.

And what was true of the Protochukchis of Central Patagonia was also true in this interesting decade of the Hypercephalonians of New Guinea, of the Malosols around North Cape, Siberia, the Microgelasmi of the Atlas Mountains, and so forth (all my own discoveries). And, on the other hand, what was true of Indianapolis and Syracuse was also true of Ogden, Utah, of Montclair, New Jersey, and so forth. The manufacture and ceremonial sanctification of the annual supply of eye salve among the Malosols, who are much given to trachoma, assumed a human significance that was utterly lacking in the problem of adequate hospitalization for the members of the National Education Association of the United States. Puberty rights among the Walarumbas of the upper Mackenzie were described with a passion quite absent in our accounts of child labor in the mill towns of the lower Connecticut. For it was the glory and charm of these primitive peoples that they had Folkways and Mores; whereas the American people had only customs and manners.

Far Away and Long Ago

As between the Protochukchis of Central Patagonia and the inhabitants of South Norwalk, Connecticut, the very slight attention accorded to the latter was not entirely due to their departure from the primitive. It was a question of space as well as time. The people of South Norwalk were not only less aboriginal than the people of Patagonia — they were several thousand miles nearer home. That constituted a formidable handicap.

We have been speaking of bathtubs. As a matter of fact, not all the inhabitants of South Norwalk are the owners or lessors of a separate family tub. In New York City there are reputed to be half a million "old-law" apartments without modern sanitary equipment. Several million American farmers manage without plumbing. In the back areas of every large American city there is a large population which in respect to housing standards — cleanliness, privacy, and quiet — harks back strongly to the primitive. There are mining villages in West Virginia that one would expect to have been eagerly seized upon by specialists in Protochukchi and Walarumba culture.

This did not happen. Twenty years ago, from the second Roosevelt administration to the first Wilson administration, the Bohunks of the Central Competitive Coal Field were a subject of enormous interest to American social students and to the general public. They are still of interest to the professional welfare workers; but for the student of civilization and for the public at large the Bohunk is obsolete. The trouble is that, living in western Pennsylvania, he is too near home.

Another instance: There was published, toward the end of the 1920's, a serious and scholarly monograph in anthropology which quickly won a large popular audience. The book was called, approximately, "On Growing Up in Nova Zembla." Among other matters it devoted considerable space to showing that boys and girls in Nova Zembla grow up with a knowledge of life that is denied to our own young people in the United States. Adolescents in Nova Zembla are spared, as one reviewer summed it up, "the horror, the shock, the nauseated recoil of our unsophisticated young when confronted with the facts of life." In Nova Zembla, individual experience begins almost with infancy. Young children are witnesses of the midwife's ministrations. They watch the preparation of the dead for burial. They spy upon lovers in the dark. In other ways they pick up the information so readily available when large numbers of people live together in cramped quarters.

Might not the American people learn something from the Nova Zemblans about educating the young in the biological fundamentals? This was obviously a legitimate and perhaps a useful question to raise. But at least one reader of the news about Nova Zembla could not help asking himself why it was necessary to go all the way to Nova Zembla. If one wanted a picture of thoroughly instructed and uninhibited child life it might be had so conveniently on Manhattan Island, west of Ninth Avenue, east of Third Avenue, north of Ninety-Sixth Street, and south of Wall Street.

Babies are all the time being born in two-room flats on Washington Street in the shadow almost of the Stock Exchange. Last rites for the dead are continually being performed in the kitchen–living-rooms of the Red Hook section of Brooklyn. Small boys go scouting at night through the hallways of the South Bronx and intrude upon intimate wooings. For scores of thousands of families in the New York of 1931, privacy is an unknown thing.

Concerning the sophisticated and thoroughly enlightened boys and girls who grow up in such an environment the welfare workers and the juvenile courts know a great deal. As in the case of the Bohunks of the Pennsylvania coal regions, these sophisticated children were a topic of intense popular concern in America before the war.

But in the decade of the 1920's the tenement children of New York, with their rich fund of information about the facts of life, were forgotten by the student of Folkways and Mores. It was, you see, merely "Growing Up in the United States."

Modes of Speech

As between the members of the Protochukchi Confederation and the inhabitants of Spokane, Washington, it was inevitable that the difference of esteem in which they were held should be reflected in a difference in literary treatment. One illustration we have already had in the case of the Protochukchi festival of capillary evacuation and the Babbitt in his warren. With certain exceptions to be noted further on, it is easy to grasp the general rule of literary composition in the 1920's. It prescribed for the primitives a tone of sustained and respectful gravity, and for the Americans a tone varying from the acid to the flip.

Thus, a Malosol medicine man in northern Siberia was invariably described with the deference, we may even say with the awe, due to an elemental force, to an original Datum of Nature. But an Episcopal bishop was something that had strayed in from the vaudeville stage. However, when it was necessary to arraign the Church as an agency of war and domestic oppression, a bishop ceased to be a clown and became a malevolent and terrifying power of darkness.

Similarly with primitive and modern club life. The weekly meetings of the Walarumba clan fraternities in their secret sweat houses were studied as a valuable contribution to our knowledge of the gregarious instinct in man. But an initiation of the Knights of the 22nd Degree at Grand Rapids, Michigan, was a performance essentially simian. However, when it was necessary to portray the small-town business man as an incubus on free intelligence in the United States, the Knights of the 22nd Degree ceased to be a gathering of subnormal playboys and took on the hideous effectiveness of an executive session of the Spanish Inquisition.

Similarly in the home. In Nova Zembla, as we have seen, the relations between parents and growing children called for the most sympathetic inquiry and appraisal. But a meeting of the Parents' Association of Dallas, Texas, was an exercise in the milder forms of imbecility.

The exceptions to this general rule of sympathy for the primitives and the loud laugh for the Americans were two: —

1. Not all writers on American civilization went in for the satirical method. There were students of American civilization who always wrote with gravity and decorum; too much so, as we shall see a little further down.

2. The jazz writers, too, acknowledged that there were certain departments of human interest in the United States which did not admit of the flip method, but demanded serious and respectful consideration.

With the reader's permission we shall first take up class 2. The literary manner of the jazz writers varied in accordance with a very simple rule. Subjects which the inhabitants of Ohio and Utah took seriously must be handled with a maximum of frivolity. On the other hand, subjects which the average American considered to be minor, trivial, or even negligible, were discussed with enormous dignity, and in a style combining the best features of Plato's Dialogues, the novels of Marcel Proust, and Secretary Mellon's report for the fiscal year ending June 30 last.

Under this rule the flippant style was prescribed for the discussion of American business, business men, cities, family life, churches, colleges, Congress, the Supreme Court, the Constitution, the Monroe Doctrine, endowments for cancer research, associations for the protection of minors, aviation, automobiles, good roads, the World War, the League of Nations, symphony orchestras in the Mississippi Valley, luncheon clubs, Florida vacations, marriage, life insurance, famine relief in China, education, and the like. On these subjects it was the rule that Jones's ideas were a travesty on the human mind and Jones's practices were comic.

Quite different was the method prescribed for such subjects as night clubs, saxophones, the burlesque stage, jazz, comic strips, prize fights, and Coney Island. Here were genuine human values with much of the authenticity of the primitive. The style took on a corresponding elevation. It was *de rigueur* in the 1920's to speak of middle-class homes as warrens, of colleges as Babbitt halls, and of bishops as smut-hounds. But in appraising Mutt and Jeff the writer could not fail to recognize with how sure a touch of genius Bud Fisher has seized upon the dualistic machinery of the Ahriman-Ormuzd motive, which derives from the Set-Osiris motive, which is only a variant of the Cain-and-Abel motive. For, in essence, Mutt is always trying to do to little Jeff what Set did to Osiris — namely, slay and dismember him.

The United States Constitution, as we have seen, was a something incurably grotesque. But in writing of Buddy Baxter and his Twenty Bouncing Beauties of Broadway Burlesk, it was strictly required that one should say, "The ecstatic explosion of Bacchic release induced by the projection, upon the Puritan-inhibited American sensorium, of two hundredweight of provocative female flesh."

What Happened to Grandma

Of the decorous writers of this period we have said that they were always dignified, on grave subjects as well as on light. Their method of approach may be illustrated by the hypothetical case of Grandmother Jones, née Perkins, of the hill country around Ridgefield, Connecticut.

Let it be remarked, in passing, that for the ultra-primitive students of civilization Grandmother Jones-Perkins had, of course, ceased to exist. To grasp her utter insignificance it was only necessary to compare her with the typical elderly woman of the Protochukchi culture level. Try to visualize this primitive Patagonian dowager going about her daily routine: perched naked on a rock in midstream on the lookout for dead fish coming down with the current; or steeping manioc roots in water for the family beer; or rubbing the young children of the tribe with lizard oil for eczema; or, perhaps at her best, an animated colorful figure in the tribal dance around the impaled war prisoner, taking her turn at him with a dull knife. With this vibrant, palpitant evocation of Beauty and Reality, compare Grandmother Jones-Perkins, with her lace collar and brooch, her zinnias and delphiniums, her knitting, her particular brand of Ceylon, her recollections of the late Henry Ward Beecher. Except as a subject for an occasional ironic thumb-nail notation, there is obviously nothing here to detain us.

For the serious student of civilization, Grandmother Jones-Perkins did exist; but only on condition that she be observed from the same point of view and described in the same vocabulary as if she were an old woman of the Protochukchis, 8000 miles and 20,000 years away from Ridgefield, Connecticut. To the decorous, conscientious student of social phenomena, Grandmother Jones-Perkins was very much worth while; provided that one might bring to bear on her the combined technique of biometrics, social dynamics, psychology, economics, and endocrinology, and in other ways encompass Grandmother with such a wealth of scientific methodology as to make her quite unrecognizable. Of her it was in order to write: —

"In the behavior-pattern dominant among the inhabitants of Southern Connecticut, the impress of the original Congregationalist-capitalistic folkways is still discernible. In this pattern the rôle of the older women of the community is legislative without being formally coercive. We may go so far as to say that the defense of the ancient New England ethos against the encroaching waves of change is almost entirely in the hands of the female members of the community rating forty-five years and over, and irrespective of marital status. For the age class just mentioned it may be even regarded as axiomatic that as between the married female and the spinster it is the latter who is the more resolute in enforcing the hereditary Calvinistic taboos in the region north of the forty-first degree North Latitude and east of the Appalachian Divide. Beltley and Oxelheimer in their monumental contribution, *Culture Patterns between the Housatonic and Block Island,* have found that among women of forty-five years and over the pulse beat is not markedly different from the ascertained norm for the Middle Atlantic States. The respiration is correspondingly uniform. The average height is five feet four and one-half inches, with no trace of a tendency to stoop such as is encountered among the mountaineers of the lower Appalachian massif. Goitre indications are negative. Housework, including light laundry but excluding table linen and sheets, consumes four and one-half hours a day. Church, including the regular three Sabbatical prayer-house exercises and such quasi-secular cultus-recreational proliferations as the strawberry festival and the church-organ benefit picnic, two hours daily. Maintenance of clan and consanguinity bonds, — writing to married daughters in California, Nova Scotia, and Detroit, — one hour weekly. The average amount of garden space in cultivation has been estimated at 250 square feet for married women, 450 square feet for spinsters, and 150 feet for widows, but varying considerably with the presence of individual art-aptitudes and specialized technological employment — piano, water colors, putting up fruit for the local market and so forth."

The fate of Grandmother Jones-Perkins in the years after the war was the fate of the whole Jones family. Ignored by the ultra-primitivists and wrapped up beyond recognition by the culture specialists, Jones, the common man of the United States Census, of Ridgefield, Connecticut, and of the New York Subway; Jones in his measurable, recorded numbers and qualities; Jones in his daily observable habits and practices; Jones with his newspapers, autos, schools, machines, and democracies, virtually ceased to exist. In his place flourished the formulas and the epigrams.

Only toward the end of the decade did people begin to suspect that life in Jones was not quite extinct. Beneath the weight of the theories, the stencils, and the wise-cracks, he went on breathing, and with the approach of the 1930's he began to thrust his head up into the light. The full rediscovery of the American Jones by serious American writers is a promise of the years ahead of us. It will be a group Jones in harmony with the Census returns, and an individual Jones resembling the man next door and across the aisle.

II

HIS NEWSPAPERS

WHAT can be more obvious and familiar than Jones's favorite newspaper? Yet see how little he is aware of what there is in his paper when he comes to talk about it. The average American male ought to know his daily paper by heart. He spends some time with it every day in the year. Six days out of seven it is twice a day. Six days a week Jones sticks up the newspaper on the breakfast table between his wife and himself, and when she asks what there is in the paper this morning he says, "Bhrumfwllff." On Sunday he is more social-minded. On that day he is perfectly ready to share the paper with the rest of the family provided he can retain about a pound and a half of reading matter for his personal consumption. There are a great many American husbands who, I am sorry to say, spend more time in intellectual communion with the evening paper than they do with their wives. And though women do not read the newspapers as much as the men do, there must be a great many mothers of grown-up sons and daughters who see more of their newspaper at night than they do of their children. How intimately the newspaper has entered into our common life is attested by the millions of papers that are every day abandoned by the reading public in subway cars, buses, and other common carriers. People are careless to that extent only with things that are inseparably a part of themselves, things they could not do without.

But how many people, when the talk turns to the Press and the Public, or the Press and the New Ethics, or the Press and the New Generation, or Public Opinion in a Democracy, or Press and Propaganda, really know enough of what is in their daily paper to justify their participation in the debate? Very few. Observe that I have said, "When the talk turns to the Press." This reservation is more than important. It is vital to the argument; it is, in fact, the whole argument. For it is with Jones and his newspapers as with Jones in so many other phases of his daily life. When Jones, so to speak, stops living and begins discussing, when he promotes his common experience to the distinction of a Problem, he loses completely his hold on the obvious. When people merely buy newspapers and read them they know quite well why they buy them and read them.

But when they find themselves embarked upon an inquiry into the Breakdown of the Press, people in nine cases out of ten will abandon the data of their everyday experience with newspapers. They will begin to talk in formulas that are in flat contradiction to such experience. Nature affords no more engrossing spectacle than that of her highest achievement, Man, continuously getting all het up about things which he knows all along are not so.

What Newspaper Men Do Not Know About Newspapers

The public by no means enjoys a monopoly in the art of misinterpreting its newspapers. The publishers and editors who make up the newspapers are all the time forgetting what it is that they put into their papers. But here again the vital distinction must be made between newspaper men unconsciously going about their normal occupations, and newspaper men very consciously participating in a symposium on "The American Press: Is It Doomed?" We publishers and editors and subordinates know very well, to the extent of our individual responsibilities, what it is we are writing and printing and publishing. In the case of the men on top, — in the case, say, of the managing editor of a big metropolitan newspaper planning next morning's paper of anywhere from thirty-six to sixty-four pages,—it is not so utterly absurd to use the term "Napoleonic" for his ability under pressure to grasp and hold a whole world and a thousand details. He sees "Gandhi in Conference with Lord Irwin," three-column head on page 1, break over to page 12, with sketch map of India showing railroads from New Delhi to Bombay. And he also sees "Mechanics Liens Filed," on page 46—hold down to two stickfuls. The managing editor knows his paper so well that a missing subhead on page 21 slaps him in the face; and in the matter of that dog who ran seventy miles without stopping, in order to rejoin his little master in Atlantic City, the managing editor gets the night editor on the telephone and wants to know why in Hades we had nothing in the first three editions about the silver collar on the dog's neck with the letters K. H. F., as described with great detail and a certain amount of smug self-satisfaction by our neighbor the *Star–Mercury*? Oh yes, the managing editor knows very well what there is in his paper, except on Sunday afternoon when he has agreed to address the Men's Club of the Second Presbyterian Church on "The Press — Is It a Blessing or a Curse?" On such occasions a palsy descends upon him, and he opens his mouth and emits a lot of shopworn superstitions.

Let us take a specific case. In a widely circulated book dealing with contemporary social belief, though not primarily with journalism, we experience a gloomy two minutes. This occurs on the page where our author picks up his morning paper, looks upon the world of to-day as mirrored in its columns, and is saddened by the picture. He reads of an anthracite strike, a price-boost conspiracy, a new Follies beauty weighing 112 pounds, a new airplane flight to Hawaii, a politician calling another politician a liar. He reads and is mournful, because "in an ordered universe there ought to be place for human experience. But is it not strange that the modern newspaper reader finds it difficult to believe that through it all there is reason, permanence, and connecting principle?"

How complete a summary has the writer here given us of the contents of his daily paper? In all frankness, a very poor summary indeed. How much has he overlooked? Well, let us say provisionally that he has omitted about 90 per cent of the physical contents of his newspaper. If we measure by significance, if we think of news revealing permanence and connecting principle, he has omitted perhaps as much as 98 per cent. How faithful a picture of the world to-day, then, has he deduced from his newspaper? My percentages speak for themselves. But before proceeding to cite in detail the extraordinary omissions into which this highly gifted observer has been betrayed, it will be of help to lay down a general proposition about newspapers, even if it does anticipate our findings to a considerable degree.

The proposition is this: An overwhelming proportion of the news in the daily newspaper is not new. It is not new in the sense that we usually attach to News.

This is not epigram, but fact. It is an elementary fact to the managing editor when he is putting tomorrow's paper together. This fundamental consideration that most news is not new guides his conduct every minute of his working day. But it deserts our good managing editor when he stands up in the Second Presbyterian Church and tries to put in a good word for his profession. Managing editors who address men's clubs, forums, and luncheon associations will of course differ in their observations, according to the type of newspaper they happen to edit and their own professional creed. But there is one thing that all managing editors say when they have their backs against the wall of the Second Presbyterian Church. Ultra-conservative or ultra-tabloid, they will say virtually: —

It is not our fault if News is news. It is not our fault if a man who runs away with another man's wife is news, but 9999 husbands who do not run away are not news. It is not our fault if a fast express running into an open draw and killing half a hundred passengers is news, but 100,000 trains arriving at their destination without mishap and on time are not news. It is not our fault that a baby born in Winsted, Connecticut, with two heads and barking like a dog is news, but a baby with only the normal per capita equipment and crying like other human babies is not news.

This is our standard reply to the standard criticism directed against the vulgarity, the inanity, the sensationalism, of which such a goodly amount creeps into the columns of the very best of us. It is the only reply available to the truly tabloid editor, reënforced perhaps by a defiant assertion that this sort of thing is what the people want, and what are you going to do about it? In the case of the high-class newspaper the plea in extenuation, as given above, is supplemented by the contention that we do print news of a better and sounder type. We do publish constructive news. It is not always murders and railroad catastrophes and wars and night-club hostesses and Al Capone and Prohibition. We give much space to the triumphs of science, to the progress of discovery, to the growth of international amity, to education, literature, art. . . .

It is a just and proper defense to make. It is a defense that might well be taken to heart by the discouraged observer who looked at his paper and saw only a world going to the dogs. But even your conservative editor has made only the feeble beginnings of a case for himself. He has overlooked 90 per cent of the evidence in his favor as immediately available in his own columns. When he pleads that it is not his fault about runaway husbands, he is very near to pleading guilty and throwing himself on the mercy of the court. He is virtually admitting that the only kind of husband mentioned in his paper is the runaway husband; the only kind of train is the runaway train which wipes out half a hundred lives; the only kind of baby in his pages is the two-headed Winsted breed.

On the Credit Side

The managing editor who conveys that impression does himself a wrong. And he fails to do himself justice because, still fighting in the last ditch up there at the Second Presbyterian, he fails to see all those forty-eight pages of his newspaper which he had so clearly before his eyes when he was making them up. An editor discussing the foibles and virtues of the Press before an audience, orally or in writing, rarely thinks beyond his first two or three pages — certainly not beyond the first two dozen pages in which he carries his new News. He overlooks the succeeding pages, — a dozen to sixty pages, — which deal with the old News that his critics would admit to be the very best kind of news.

For instance: —

Being born is a very ancient human interest and occupation. It has only gained in prestige as it has grown rarer in recent times. The daily paper has a great deal to say about population increase: in the paid birth announcements; in the unpaid items of the Society columns; in the stories dealing with our success in cutting down infant mortality; and, by indirection, in the school pages and other pages of which we shall take note further down. When the editor pleads that a two-headed baby is news, but a normal baby is not news, he is traducing his paper. He has all kinds of news about normal babies scattered through the pages.

Being married is an ancient and still very important interest. The newspapers have their paid marriage announcements. Of far greater moment is marriage in the Society columns. Have you ever seen in the newspapers the picture of a bride and groom walking down the church steps? Have you ever encountered in a newspaper the names of those present in church and later at the reception? But, for that matter, the entire subject of Society News, so amply covered in the newspapers, may be regarded as primarily dedicated to, and culminating in, marriage. Palm Beach and Aiken, Newport and Junior League and the Larchmont Yacht races — they are all the preliminary to that picture of bride and groom walking down the church steps, if the present writer knows his W. M. Thackeray.

Dying is an important item in people's lives. We in the newspaper business hear that the very first thing to which a great many people turn in the morning paper is the obituary columns.

Buying and selling is a deep-rooted human institution; and the newspaper may devote to Business a solid dozen pages or more out of a paper of forty-eight pages. And this is not the dramatic first-page business news of Wall Street Crashes, or the Romances of Business in which two Middle Western brothers rise from small beginnings to the command of a railroad empire, or the crimes of business as catalogued by Senators Brookhart, Norris, and Borah. The dozen solid pages of business which the paper carries day after day are concerned with the far more absorbing business — absorbing to 99 per cent of business men — which deals with the number of bags of coffee on the docks at Santos, the unfilled orders in the United States Steel Corporation, and those supremely fascinating lists and tables which end their daily tale with the Final Closing Prices.

Labor and wages are subjects of considerable interest to considerable millions of people; and there is news about labor and wages in pages that people never mention when speaking before the men's club of the Second Presbyterian. Let me assure you that the news contained in the Help Wanted columns of our papers is very poignant news indeed.

Play is supposed to count for something in American life; and I am told that if one looked hard enough he could find sporting pages in American newspapers.

So much by way of a preliminary hint concerning the number of things in the newspaper of which our discouraged observer, as cited above, apparently failed to take notice. Let us now look into the matter a little more intensively. For this purpose the reader of the present lines is invited kindly to pick up his paper and follow directions.

What's in the Paper To-day?

To-day's issue of our favorite morning paper happens to be fifty-two pages big. For a reason which will soon become apparent, the reader is requested to start turning the pages, not with page 1, but with page 52, and to move backward to the first page. Now right at the start, that is to say on the last page, we are confronted with a newspaper item which is very rarely mentioned in discussions before the Interurban Forum on "The Press: Does It Truly Mirror Life?" The thing I refer to is an Advertisement. We shall encounter a great many others as we move on through the pages. Indeed, it may be taken as fact, on this writer's word, that the advertisements will account for about one half of the entire paper. In this issue of fifty-two pages there will be twenty-five pages of advertising, or more.

Page 52, then, with which we start on our journey into the terra incognita of the morning paper that you have read all your life, and your father before you for a good many years — page 52 is mostly or perhaps entirely advertising. So we turn it over, and on page 51 our eyes light on a heading in big black type several columns wide, "Shipping and Mails." Have you ever heard of anyone wanting to know at what hour the *Barataria* from Cherbourg and Southampton is expected at her pier? Or at what hour the post closes for the *Didactic,* carrying mails to Stockholm and Helsingfors? Or do the Havana boats sail from the North River or the East River? Or when should a letter be posted so as to catch the air mail for Atlanta? But have you ever heard any publicist, or men's club, or editor on the defensive, discuss the Degradation of the Ship News?

Backing away from page 51, we pass through three solid pages devoted to what is known in the trade as "Classified Ads." These are small advertising notices of a few lines each without a separate head, but grouped under a general classification: Help Wanted Female, Furnished Rooms, Country Board, and the like. In the trade all advertisements are either "Classified" or "Display." The latter are the prominent, individual advertisements, often of full-page size and amply described by their name. Through these three pages of Classified, then, we speed and so arrive at page 47 — Real Estate. Here is news, with or without advertising, of realty sales, rentals, building projects, and the like. You have probably heard of people who are thinking of a new apartment next October, or perhaps of buying that little place in the country. But have you ever heard of any minister preaching on "The Influence of Second-Mortgage Interest Rates on the Morals of the Young Generation"?

Moving backwards in our remorseless course, we pass through a couple of pages devoted to subjects of which the discussion forums have never even dreamed as existing in their newspapers — police department orders and assignments, teachers' licenses, army and navy orders and assignments, wills and probate, liens filed, judgments satisfied, the Weather . . .

The Weather! We of the newspapers are attacked for pandering to vulgarity and vacuity and pruriency and other low instincts. But never do we get credit for supplying millions of readers day after day with clean entertainment and instruction in this one instance of the weather. Yes, most of us are all for naval conferences and unemployment solutions and municipal good government, and other worth-while news; but we are apt to forget that on any one day, certainly in the absence of a first-rate international crisis, there are ever so many more people interested in the temperature record of the last twenty-four hours, the barometric pressure, the precipitation in inches, the direction and velocity of the wind, and, of course, the forecast for the next twenty-four hours. In New York City, in Boston, in Los Angeles, I will vouch that on any non-winter day there are fewer people intimately concerned over Franco-Italian naval rivalry than there are fishermen wanting to know when it is high tide at Sandy Hook, or wherever it is near Boston and Los Angeles that you keep your High Water and Low Water.

It was the Weather that unquestionably brought human speech into existence when anthropoid Number 1 finally succumbed to the urge to convey to anthropoid Number 2 his firm conviction that it would never stop raining. The Weather still exercises its irresistible spell over most of us, and particularly those of us who are on the shady side of sixty. The next time you are in mixed company try mentioning Naval Disarmament and observe the response. Then mention the fact that winters are not so cold as they used to be and see what happens. When we newspapers bow our heads, bloody under the bludgeonings of our crime news and our sex news and our movie-chatter news, does a good Samaritan ever pause to lend us as much as a kind word for the sake of the Weather News we print? Yet daily we celebrate the fresh clean winds and rains, the surge of the sea at High or Low Water, as the case may be, the heartening sweep of plains and mountains, vast areas of High and Low Pressure, forests and lakes and river valleys, the good dry air of Abilene, Kansas, where it is 110 in the shade, the challenge of Medicine Hat, Alberta, where it is 35 below — all the freedoms, all the purities. . . .

But we must really tear ourselves away, for there is still a big paper ahead of us. We leave the Weather somewhere, say about page 45, and immediately land in the Business pages. Business: stock market, bond market, grain, hogs, sugar, coffee, railroad, foreign exchange — we pass through ten pages of Business News, of which you hear nothing in the discussion forums, and so are on page 35.

On page 35 a heavy black headline all the way across the page, known in the trade as a "Streamer," takes note of what the A's did to the Red Sox in the tenth, and so steadily back to page 31 where the sport news begins. Beyond that:—

2 pages of theatre, music, movie and radio, to page 29.

2 pages of what the public and the discussion forums accept as news; it is both sober and sensational, a Torch Murder and a Job Stabilization Plan, to page 27.

1 page of advertising.

1 page of obituaries, births, engagements, both as news items and as paid notices.

1 editorial page.

2 pages of Society news. And finally, all the way back to page 1—

21 pages of news and advertising, the equivalent, say, of ten pages of News, new News; the News discussed in that celebrated symposium, "Our Press: Mentor or Menace?"

In this issue of our morning paper, a perfectly

typical issue, the pages from which our discouraged observer derived his picture of a sad world would be at most twelve pages out of a total of fifty-two pages, or say 25 per cent of the contents of the newspaper. Actually the proportion is much smaller. For if you insist on thinking that News is only the new News, the highly dramatic, the exceptional, the unforeseen, then by far the greater part of that dozen of News pages is not News. For even those pages contain a great deal of the routine and familiar: prohibition, city budgets, telephone rates, traffic regulations, and not at all the wars and crimes and seditions connoted by real News. My original estimate was that our observer allowed himself to be discouraged by 10 per cent of the contents of his newspaper and forgot the other 90 per cent. This estimate would now be confirmed by our detailed examination.

The Customer Is Right

But at this point — and let us hope not until this point — the reader of these lines is likely to exhibit more than a touch of impatience. "This is all very clever," he may remark, "and very professional and authoritative and all that. But the great majority of us are not editors or professors of journalism or publicists, and we do not go in for spectroscope analysis and test-tube refinements. We know what we mean by News, and in spite of all your ingenious little arguments, News is not the weather yesterday at 3 P. M., or that Schroeder beat De la Fuentes for the 18.1 inch running-high breast stroke championship. At least it is not News in the sense that the conquest of unemployment or our adherence to the World Court is News."

But that, of course, is begging the question. We are not dealing with the intrinsic importance of different classes of news. We are concerned with the question whether or not the American newspaper reflects the whole life of the whole American people, and I have tried to show that it does; and instead of resorting to wire-drawn technicalities I have only been setting down the obvious. These obvious facts about what people read, and how, are regularly overlooked by the social observers who would see life through only 10 per cent of the contents of the newspaper. Did I say 10 per cent? It was not the only estimate I made at the beginning of this paper. I said that people in discussing the newspaper forget 90 per cent of its contents as measured in space, and 98 per cent of its contents as measured in "reader interest." It is not my fault that people read the weather news or the lists from Palm Beach and Greenbrier or the names of the wedding guests with a sense of intense participation that is much more rarely evoked by the news from Geneva or from the Farm Board.

Let us put it bluntly: Except for some highly sensational murder or romance or impending war cloud on the first page, even that first page seldom evokes the direct interest with which the Wall Street man turns to his stock-exchange reports, the realty man to his real-estate pages, and most of us to the sporting pages, and the wedding pages, and the obituary pages. Day in, day out, the vast bulk of "reader interest" goes out, not to the front page, but to the inside pages. This is not technical or academic argumentation. It is simple fact. It is one of the numerous obvious facts which get themselves forgotten in American life, but which we can recover by pausing for a little while, and shaking off the formulas from our minds, and consulting the data of our own common experience and practice.

Supplementing the data of your own experience are the findings of the experts. I am not an adorer of the Questionnaire as an instrument of the Truth, but we cannot overlook the uniform results of numerous questionnaires, inquiries, researches, into this problem of what people read and why. Such inquiries have been made by the newspapers themselves, by the schools of journalism, by the advertising agencies, by miscellaneous sociologists. With some human variation the answers to the question, How do you read your daily paper? would be as follows:—

The Business Man: He glances at the headlines on the front page, then turns to the financial pages. In the course of the day, quite often in the evening, he manages to get some time for the general news.

The Professional Man: Surprisingly like the Business Man.

The White-Collar Man (in the great majority): He glances through the headlines on the front page, then turns to the sporting pages.

The Manual Worker (in the vast majority): He does not even look over the front-page headlines, but turns to the sporting pages.

The Housewife (higher income class): She turns to the social activities, the department-store advertising, and the general vital statistics — obituaries, weddings, and so forth. Sometimes she glances at the headlines on the first page.

The Housewife (lower income classes): She turns immediately to the serial love story and then to the housekeeping pages.

The Shop Girl and the Factory Girl: The serial

story and the heart-interest news and movie news. It is stated in the trade that 75 per cent of all women readers are consumers of serial stories and heart-interest features.

And that is what I meant by saying that the bulk of the news, and the most interesting news in the sense of coming closest to the hearts of the greatest number of people, is the news that is not new. That is to say, it is mostly new and fresh, of course, but it is the new day's version of old things: the new stock-market quotations about an old commodity called Railroads; the new prices of familiar things like coffee and sugar; the new arrivals and departures of familiar ships traveling on preëstablished schedules; the new births and marriages and deaths; the new standing of the old baseball clubs, the new bit of advice — in your evening paper — to the new mother, and to the vegetarian cook, and to the troubled parent of difficult children — new phases of the old stuff, as old as the hills. That is what fills up most of the paper. And therefore when you pick up the paper and see that there is famine in China and an impasse at the naval conference and a shooting of bootleggers by prohibition officers, or of citizens by gangsters, and you say, "What a terrible world this is," you simply have n't read your newspaper.

The Life of the People

Our managing editor, fighting a desperate rear-guard action up there at the Second Presbyterian Church, has read his paper; he read it before it was made up. But in the stress of debate, amid the crash of heavy formulas and flaring superstitions, the poor fellow forgets all the good, wholesome, quiet, simple, fundamental things he has put into his paper this morning. He asks plaintively if it is his fault that runaway husbands are news and stay-at-home husbands are not news. But as a matter of fact the 9999 husbands who have not run away are all over this morning's newspaper. You will find the decent, loyal, non-fugitive husband in the Situations Wanted, Male, where he is looking for a job to support the wife and young whom he has not abandoned. You will find him frequently, one is glad to see, in the Help Wanted columns, where he is inquiring for assistance in the nice little business he has built up, to the point where both the girl and the boy (whom he has not deserted) are sure of going to college. You will find the decent undramatic husband in the news items from the Board of Health; for I take it that a steady decline in infant mortality signifies that heads of families as a rule do not desert their wives and babies, but stay at home and see to it that there is enough good food in the house for the nursing mother, and later that there is enough fresh pasteurized milk for the baby.

Where in the newspapers are the 100,000 trains that do not run into an open draw and kill half a hundred people? They are all over the paper: in the confidence with which a man steps on board the train in Boston knowing that a little more than three days later — and in fact to the minute — he will be in San Francisco; in the advertised presentment of the beautiful movie queens and strong captains of industry who are all the time traveling on those splendid Limiteds and Fliers and Arrows and Clippers; in the steel-mill figures for rail production for the week ending May 5; in the figures for freight-car loadings — figures so impressive as to indicate that surely now and then a freight train does get through without being smashed up by a crack passenger flier; in the Government Ownership problem — or why should Senator Norris want to take over the railroads if all they do is to get wrecked; in the stock-market quotations — or why should anyone be paying real money for shares in New York Central, "Pennsy," and New Haven, if all they did was to run trains into Long Island Sound and the Delaware River and drown people?

Where in the newspaper are the 9,999,999 babies out of ten million who are not born with two heads and a bark? They are all over the place: in the company of the non-runaway fathers of whom I have already spoken; in the company of their non-abandoned mothers traveling on some of these non-catastrophic trains and ships which I have just mentioned; in the reports of a new school year in New York City and a million children registered; in the story of 5,000,000 boys and girls in the high schools and nearly a million young women and men in the colleges. . . .

Take the Sunday rotogravure pictures of these American children, with their football and their hockey and their baseball and their tennis and their sprinting and their high-jumping and their recreation parks and athletic meets in the heart of the tenement districts — in those rotogravure pictures how many two-headed boys and seven-toed girls have you met? "It is not my fault," says the managing editor, "if one-headed, two-legged, five-toed, robust, pink-cheeked children are not News." And he prints a picture of 10,000 little Czechoslovakian girls in white blouses and blue skirts doing gymnastic exercises in honor of President Masaryk. That picture elicits from countless American woman readers outcries of "Darling!" Then they go to the Discussion Club and ask, "Why do newspapers show only the seamy side of life?"

It is not my fault, says the editor, if the normal and the routine are not news; and so hands over half his paper — 10 pages out of 20, 25 pages out of 50, 90 pages out of 180 on Sunday — to Advertisements, which are concerned exclusively with the normal, the routine: the new spring suit, the new fur coat, the new refrigerator, the new apartment. These advertisements are close kin to the news stories about the coffee market and the bond market and the real-estate market and are, like them, unsensational, fundamental, concerned with things that need not be apologized for.

It is a very big subject in itself — Advertising — and one we may have to take up elsewhere. It is enough here to point out how utterly unaware are writers on the Press of the great, normal, sane, pleasant world revealed in the advertising columns. It is a world of houses, lands, food, clothes, schools, travel, automobiles, radio. You very seldom see an advertisement offering a five-room apartment guaranteed to collapse and kill the tenants. You do not find the New Haven Railroad promising, if you will take the Merchant's Limited, to run it off the rails for you near New London. You do not find gangsters offering, in the Classified Ads, for $50 a head to take your enemies for a ride, and furnish their own guns and taxis. You do not even find department stores suddenly going sensational and offering $29.50 dresses for $57.00. No, in the advertising pages everything is normal; they make up half the contents of our newspapers; and people forget them when the question before us this afternoon is "The Press: Is It Worth Saving?"

III

HIS OPINIONS AND HIS POLITICS

WHEN Herbert Hoover defeated Alfred E. Smith in November 1928 by a popular vote of 21 millions to 15 millions, by 444 electoral votes to 87, by 40 states to 8, and incidentally wrenched from the palpitating flesh of the Solid South the fair states of Virginia, North Carolina, Florida, and Texas, if only pro tem. — when Herbert Hoover did all these things to Alfred E. Smith with the most consummate ease in the world for the reason that said Smith is a Roman Catholic, there was signally vindicated the dignity of the average American man as against our specialists in Mass Behavior and Public Opinion.

Upon the meaning of the last Presidential election there cannot be, and as a matter of fact there has not been, any serious difference of opinion. Everybody agrees that in November 1928 there took place in these United States a popular uprising against the Pope. A great many people rejoice in the event and call it a popular upheaval in defense of free

Protestant America. A great many people deplore the event and describe it as an upflare of bigotry and hate. For our present purpose the two explanations are exactly the same. They agree in asserting that the last election showed more than thirty million Americans terribly in earnest. And when I see the dignity of the average man vindicated by the vote against Al Smith, — or for him, — I mean only the obvious: that a bigot is a more dignified and impressive object than a ventriloquist's dummy. For it is precisely to the level of the dummy on the knee of the vaudeville artist, the jumping jack at the end of the wire, the scarecrow flapping at the will of the winds, that the average American voter had been reduced by the specialists in public opinion who worship at the shrine of Propaganda.

It is the essential doctrine in this propaganda explanation of mass behavior that the way in which ordinary men think is determined for them by a few shrewd people on top who have managed to obtain control of the newspapers and the radios in the current fiscal year. It is a parallel doctrine that the way in which the millions vote is determined by what they have read in the newspapers or in the campaign literature or heard from the platform or over the radio during the last few weeks before election day. It is a doctrine passionately held that the political party which in the summer of a Presidential year controls the greatest number of newspapers and the largest campaign fund will win the election. This it will do by persuading, converting or bamboozling a majority of the voters.

Public Opinion in the Levant

The propaganda theory of human conduct, as it flourished in the last decade, thus made it possible to solve a great many puzzles which had perplexed the psychologists and observers of earlier times. Try to think of some man who felt very strongly about some other man — well, let us take the way Shylock felt about Antonio. The propaganda theory makes it all as clear as daylight. Shylock hated Antonio because of what he had read and what he had heard about the merchant of Venice. The Jew, as is well known, was an assiduous patron of the *Rialto Evening Graphic,* and in that lively sheet he was continually being regaled with pungent gossip about Antonio's private life as a member of the Venetian smart set. Shylock was a subscriber to the *Lido Gazette,* a weekly journal of serious social criticism. There he encountered many a caustic analysis of the business methods of Venice's merchant princes, among whom Antonio figured prominently. Shylock often read in the *Adriatic Monthly* well-considered articles dealing with the longer trends in Venetian life, and in these the name of Antonio would frequently occur, not always in the most favorable light. By numerous other vents and channels Shylock was exposed to the sustained pressure of the anti-Antonio propagandists, lobbyists, press agents, and counsels on public relations; so that we may say of this Jew of Venice that his conspicuously neutral, insipid, and featureless soul provided a clean slate for the experts in human manipulation to write on. Any fifty-ducat-a-week ink slinger in Venice could do what he pleased with Shylock.

Yes; Shylock hated Antonio wholly because of what he had read and been told about Antonio, and not because he, Shylock, had eyes, hands, dimensions, affections, passions. Your true-blue propagandist will entirely overlook, or else dismiss as irrelevant, the circumstance that if you tickled Shylock he laughed without any suggestion from the newspapers, and if you pricked him he bled without any editorial guidance. Always this Jew of Venice was being swayed by the gossip paragraphs in the *St. Mark's Weekly* and the *Levantine Review,* and never by the fact that Antonio had interfered with his livelihood and spat upon his gaberdine.

And that, apparently, is what happened in the United States in the year 1928. When the four

Southern states made their stand against the Pope, it must have been because the propagandists in the course of the summer campaign put it into people's minds that a Roman Catholic ought not to be President. Had it not been for the press agents, the Protestant South would just as lief have voted for a Roman Catholic, having inherited a perfectly open mind on the subject from their fathers, who had it from *their* fathers. If voters in the South marked their ballots against the Inquisition, and against the fires of Smithfield, and against Louis XIV's treatment of the Huguenots, and against James II and for William of Orange, and in short against the Scarlet Woman of Rome and in defense of the little white church on the village green — when they did all these things, it was because the propagandists put notions into their heads, and not because of anything they felt and feared on their own account.

But, on second thought, this could not be. For it appears that the secession of half the solid South from Alfred E. Smith in 1928 was a surrender to bigotry; and plainly a bigot cannot be a puppet. A bigot has eyes, hands, dimensions, organs, affections, and passions. They are affections and passions so strong that his eyes may go bloodshot, and his hands itch to get at your throat. Propaganda, in the sense in which men used the word before it became a post-Armistice fetish, can indeed play upon the bigot. Propaganda can minister to his fears, rouse his jealousies, fan his dormant hatreds. But that is not the propaganda which the decade of the 1920's had in mind. Propaganda then was the omnipotent agency that could do with the puppet man what it pleased. In theory, and for the wilder votaries in practice, propaganda could make Texas and Alabama vote for the Pope by the expenditure of enough money on speakers, "literature," newspapers, and radio. Propaganda, as the decade used the word, denied that man is filled with hate or with memories or with fears or with anything. Man is an empty vessel into which the dispenser can pour whatever brew he pleases. But the 1928 election reminded the would-be pourers that the vessel, Man, is really filled with strange juices and compounds and prejudices, dating back some seventy years to the Civil War, a hundred and fifty years to the Revolutionary War, four hundred years to Luther and the Armada, and so an indefinite number of thousands and thousands of years back to the cave and the tree hut.

Odd Discrepancy

And yet here is an odd thing. Parallel to this doctrine of propaganda which teaches that the mass of men are putty with which you may do anything, there ran through this decade of the 1920's the other doctrine that the mass of men are clods with which you can do nothing. Did I say parallel? These mutually destructive appraisals were frequently encountered hand in hand in the same observer, in the same book. A thread which the reader will find running through these remarks of mine is the shrieking inconsistencies and contradictions of the trained mind of our time when it contemplates the average man. The student of civilization contemplates the resident of Tenth Avenue, and finds him to be now this and now remarkably the opposite of this. . . .

Well, that is proper enough. Man has always been known as the creature in whom at any one moment you may find both this and the opposite of this. But it is the peculiar mark of the intellectual temper of our time that it denies to the average man the complicated soul structure of which we are a bit more than proud in our own educated selves. The average man must be wholly one thing, and now he must be wholly the opposite thing, depending on what particular formula I, the educated observer, have momentarily fallen in love with. For it has been the basic rule for the study of mankind in our days that we shall not look at common men and observe how they change under our eyes. The thing to watch is the formulas about common men. When a formula has served its purpose or lost its novelty we can look about for another formula. At no time is it essential to take a look at Jones.

Thus it happened, in the years after the war, that the average man was a man of granite, and also a man of straw, according to convenience. If you wished to express disapproval of the average man's aversion to experiment and progress you spoke of him as the slave of hereditary superstitions. He was a man chained to his taboos. He was a creature dominated by fears. He was the terrorized victim of his Medicine Men and his Old Men of the Tribe. Their vested interests required that the average man stay put, and he has learned the lesson so well that civilization consists of the mass of mankind being dragged forward against its will.

But the very next day, and sometimes on the very next page, this human clod, this sodden product of priestly taboos and terrors and superstitions, this dull, immobile brute entity, becomes, by the theory of propaganda, the most airy, fairy, gossamer thing imaginable. He becomes Mob. He becomes Herd. He becomes Puppet. Anyone can twist him around his finger. Anyone can make him go wherever he wishes. The clod with whom you could do nothing becomes the manikin with whom you may do any-thing. Which it will be depends entirely on which formula is indicated at the moment — the formula that man is fettered by taboos or the formula that man is ruled by propaganda.

What no self-respecting formula will admit is that both things might simultaneously be true of the average man; that he is a creature slow to move and easy to move, lumpish and impulsive, easily duped and with a millennial wisdom of his own; a clod with a spark at the heart of it. That the average man is a complex man rarely enters the formulas of the intellectualist observer, because formulas, to be beautiful, must be simple. They must fall pat. They must answer everything, without hesitation or reservation. Only in that way can a formula become eminently quotable in printed gossip and polite conversation.

They Killed Him with Kindness

One possible misconstruction I am anxious to avoid. When I speak of the educated observer and his fondness for describing the common man as a puppet I am far from arguing that the motive behind the act is always contempt or dislike. Very often the impulse behind the puppet theory is commiseration. There is present the wish to make excuses for the common man. How, the educated observer asks himself, shall I explain the extraordinary fact that a majority of the American people acquiesce in or even support a world war of which I, the serious student, heartily disapprove? How shall I explain the division of the American people into political parties which have ceased to have any real meaning for me? Or, taking a problem on which there can be no difference of opinion, how shall we explain the toleration of municipal misgovernment by millions of Americans? How shall we explain the upflare of ugly passions — religious, racial, regional — in these United States?

The answer that springs from contempt and dislike is the answer given by the H. L. Mencken school of anti-democratic thought. Of course it is not a new school. It is part of the old tradition which holds that mankind is incurably bestial. Here the answer to war and municipal misgovernment and religious bigotry and censorship and the rest is simple. The great majority of men are vicious, cruel, cowardly, gluttonous, lecherous, superstitious. But, chief of all, the mass of men are envious of superior status and superior merit and ever ready to favor the lower against the higher. The democracy is a herd of grunting and rooting swine.

Prohibition, for instance, offers no puzzle to Mr. Mencken. It was put over on the American people by the yokels of the back country whose convivial pleasures are restricted to swilling raw gin and hugging the blowzy kitchenmaid behind the barn. This uncouth herd saw to it that the city "feller" shall not drink civilized liquor in pleasant dining rooms and in the company of charming women. Things in this country are the way they are for the reason that the great majority of the American people are disgusting animals.

But this is precisely the view against which the usual educated observer strongly protests. He wants to believe in democracy. He believes in the decency and good intentions of the average man. Under the circumstances, what other explanation can there be, whenever the common man goes astray, than to suggest that he has been misinformed, misled, deceived, betrayed? The common man does not want war. He is always dragged into war by his leaders for their own selfish ends. The common man in Virginia is not by nature Democratic, or in Vermont by nature Republican. That is only a vicious state of things inaugurated by chance but perpetuated by the politicians. The common man wants a much better type of Presidential candidate than he is getting. The nominees are "put over" by the Interests, who are notorious for their control of the machinery of both parties. It is not necessary to go into details. As against the Menckenites, who hold with old Thomas Hobbes that man is hopelessly brutish, we have the idealists defending the Jean Jacques Rousseau man, who is by nature and intentions altogether admirable, but is the victim of forces outside himself.

And yet in the final account much the harsher sentence upon the common man is pronounced, not by the "roughneck" Menckenites, but by the kindly and well-meaning idealists. The most familiar contribution by Mr. Mencken to the American vocabulary and to American thought is the Boob. But as a matter of fact Mr. Mencken does not in the least think of his archenemy as a boob. A boob is a ninny with whom you can amuse yourself to your heart's content. A boob is a dolt with whom you can do what you like. A boob is the fellow to whom you sell a season's ticket for the Brooklyn Bridge or the Congressional Library. A boob, in short, is somebody whom you can notice when you choose and disregard when you have lost interest. But what are the facts about Mr. Mencken's Boob? Mr. Mencken does not twist the Boob around his fingers. It is the Boob who twists Mr. Mencken around his own uncouth fingers, by the Baltimore editor's own confession. It is the Boob that compels Mr. Mencken and the rest of us to dance to his own clownish piping.

If a boob is something ridiculous and ineffective, how can the name apply to the creature whom the Nietzschean school concedes to be in control of America? He imposes censorships and prohibitions. He dominates the legislatures which dominate the universities. He sets the standard for art and thought and taste. The Mencken yokel is not in the least a yokel, because he is not under anybody's yoke; it is Mr. Mencken who is under the yokel's yoke. The yokel is the confessed master. And Mr. Mencken on democracy is not thinking in the least of a collection of oafs and dolts. He is thinking of a mob of ravening wolves.

The Real Enemy

Rather is it the idealist friends of democracy that have made a boob of the common man, with the kindliest intentions. They look out on a world in which many things are amiss, and in order to absolve the common man from responsibility for this sad state of things they come dangerously near to adopting the methods of the successful criminal lawyer who obtains acquittals in murder trials by proving that his client is a victim of *dementia præcox*. Mr. Mencken pays the common American man the enormous compliment of regarding him as a dangerous fanatic, as a Force. But the would-be friends of the common man have reduced him to a nonentity.

In their accounts it regularly appears that the great majority of mankind are dolls dancing to hidden wires — vocal dolls whose powers of utterance are restricted to saying "War," "Peace," "Country," "Flag," in response to pressure applied at a point near the stomach or the heart; primitive intelligences who believe everything they are told to believe, and nothing else; primitive emotional machines which feel whatever the engineer that presses the button wants them to feel, and nothing else.

That the emotions of the common man may be fairly spontaneous and genuine, that his thoughts may be based in part at least on his inalienable human experience, that his acts may be dictated by something deserving the name of reason — such possibilities hardly enter into the evaluations of man as puppet. Here is a typical summation of the propaganda doctrine of human conduct as it flourished in the 1920's: —

The range of subjects upon which men are fitted to form original opinions is very narrow. Most men are obliged to accept the opinion of someone having prestige in politics, in religion, in science, in morals. This is unavoidable, since it is possible for the average man to be expert only in the small field of his regular occupation.

And what, as a matter of fact, is the "small field of his regular occupation," outside of which the average man is precluded from framing judgments of his own? The average man's occupation consists merely in being born, growing up, earning his living by his labor, marrying a wife and trying to make a success of it, raising children and trying to understand them and get himself understood by them, affiliating himself with a church, a trade-union, a chamber of commerce, a life-insurance company, a fraternal order, enjoying good wages and resenting unemployment, finding out that food is good and lack of it is bad, seeing the sun rise in the morning and set at night, watching his son march off to war and, let us hope, return unharmed. The field of the average man's regular occupation is restricted to the business of actor and spectator in the parade of life and death, of laughter and tears, and of the two and two that make four. This is all that enters into the average man's range of intelligence and emotion.

One thing there is obviously in common between the Mencken interpretation of Man the Wolf and the kindlier interpretation of man as puppet. Both views arise out of the sense of amazement, with or without indignation, that the common man should insist on being what he is, instead of being what I, the Superman, or I, the Idealist, think the common man ought to be at this precise moment.

Have You Heard the Latest?

So much, then, for the sense in which Mr. Hoover's victory over Governor Smith in 1928 vindicated the dignity of the average man. A bigot has more human value than a marionette. A good hater is more impressive than an empty meal sack. Caliban is a richer personality than Simple Simon. It remains only to ask in whose eyes the average man was vindicated. And the answer, again, is in the eyes of the intellectual observers; for it is not to be denied that the 1928 election taught them something.

It is the peculiar quality of this type of men that it requires an upheaval, or an eruption, or a cataclysm, or at the very least a hot Presidential election to draw their attention to the existence of things of which we ordinary men are aware by looking at our neighbors and in the newspaper. Suppose, for instance, that the existing tension between Argentina and the United States, arising from our tariff on Argentinian meat products, should develop into a crisis. This crisis would come to some of our social idealists as a startling reminder that millions of Americans have bacon and eggs for breakfast.

In this manner the popular triumph of Colonel Lindbergh came to some of our social students as a startling reminder that hero worship is not dead among the American people. You see, they had seen it so often stated in magazine articles and in books that this is an age of skepticism and disillusion. They had omitted to take note of one hundred and eighteen million Americans who plainly were not disillusioned or skeptical. Apparently they had not heard of Babe Ruth.

In this manner the publication of official figures showing that life insurance in force in the United States in the year 1930 amounted to nearly one hundred billion dollars came to students of civilization as a startling reminder that family affection and responsibility are not dead in the United States. The student of American civilization was too busy elsewhere to take note that life insurance was growing at an amazing rate. And of course he was too busy to inform himself by personal observation that in the year 1930 men were still concerned about the future of their wives and children in case anything happened to the head of the family. The student of civilization had read so much about the Break–Up of the Family that it came as a surprise to find in the year 1930 families still in operation.

In this manner a play called *The Green Pastures*

came in March 1930 as an almost catastrophic reminder that there were still alive in New York a considerable number of people susceptible to the old-fashioned emotions and pieties and traditions. The student of civilization had become so deeply absorbed in his own formulas about the Moral Revolution and the Collapse of Standards that he had forgotten to take note of several million people in New York City who were but imperfectly sophisticated or hard-boiled.

All these startling reminders were necessary because observers of mankind had forgotten to look at their fellow men with the eyes of fellows and of simple men. You looked at Jones exclusively in terms of Revolution or New Ages or Herd Instincts or Glands, or whatever was the latest combination of capital letters, in which alone the Truth resided. You satirized Jones, or flayed him, or debunked him, or psychoanalyzed him, or extracted his teeth for focal infections, or put him under the X-ray and the ultra-violet and the infra-red, or looked at him in the manner suggested by H. G. Wells, through the magnifying glass which distorts while it enlarges, or photographed him in his Rotarian garments and in his atavistic reversions and his sexual neuroses — but you had no time to take note that crowds adore heroes and mothers love babies and people are fond of bacon and eggs for breakfast. Such methods of observation were too direct and too commonplace.

Postscript on Advertising

Now the vogue of propaganda as the explanation of American mass behavior is due to all of us in general, and to one interest in particular.

We all suffer, though in different degree, from the inability to understand how in the world it is possible for anyone not to think as we do on any given subject. The only way in which such extraordinary conduct on the part of the other man can be accounted for, assuming that the poor fellow is not insane, is propaganda. Some external compulsion has interfered with the ordinary course of nature when Jones refuses to share our views. We are all like that; and the less we see of Jones in the body, the more we are like that.

The particular interest that has contributed to the prestige of propaganda is the complex of occupations, professions, and trades that may be grouped under the general head of Advertising.

It is not quite a subject for surprise when advertising agents and agencies, publicity managers, goodwill promoters, directors of campaigns and drives, salute with something more than satisfaction the doctrine that people can be taught always to do what they are told; that people indeed do only what they are told — provided one uses up in the telling enough white paper in the newspapers and magazines, enough pine boarding on the highways, enough electric current along the Great White Ways of the big cities. Yes, my friends, strange as it may seem, it is the professionals of publicity who most ardently testify to the irresistible efficacy of propaganda. They have even written books about it.

The efforts of the Grand Dukes of Publicity have been reënforced by one particular subdivision of the general class of All of Us mentioned a few lines back. I refer to the progressive economists and sociologists who disapprove of so many features of our business civilization. With them a favorite topic is the wastefulness of American business methods and especially the waste of advertising.

But mind you, when critics speak of the waste of advertising they do not mean that it is waste because advertising fails to make men do things or buy things. On the contrary, it is the heart of their case that advertising makes men do things they should not and buy many more things than they need or than is good for them. It is their contention that anybody who starts out with an advertising appropriation of $5,000,000 can make the American people buy anything, wear anything, eat anything, read anything, ride about in anything, smoke anything, believe anything.

Does this hideous charge arouse bitter indignation in the ranks of the advertising business? It does not. Perhaps it hurts a bit — in one's abstract after-business hours — to be accused of making people spend their money needlessly. But how helpful it is to the advertising business to be constantly so accused! How conducive it is to the encouragement of new $5,000,000 accounts from manufacturers desirous of imposing a little more waste on the American people!

And what is the more prosaic, less Napoleonic, truth about advertising — about its effectiveness in shaping men's lives and bank accounts in these United States, about its adequacy as a central explanation of American behavior? The truth about advertising is in kind the same as the truth about propaganda, though we may note a difference in degree. The printed advertisement is unquestionably more effective in shaping the buying behavior of the American people than are the propaganda headlines in shaping the nation's thinking and conduct. But the doctrine of an irresistible Advertiser having his own way with the buying public is nonsense.

That is to say: —

Advertising may induce a few people to buy frequently what they do not need and induce a great many people to buy occasionally what they do not need. But the number of such victims is small in the entire mass of consumers and the entire volume of the nation's business.

Advertising may succeed in forcing a novelty down the public's throat and into commercial success. But such achievements are trivial when compared with the vast body of commercial success based on sound human needs, mass movements, epochal changes, new turns in civilization.

You see so much automobile advertising about you, in the newpapers, magazines, on the road, in the window displays, that it has become a commonplace for students of the national civilization to say that Americans ride in automobiles because the advertisers make them.

But it is a commonplace that Henry Ford succeeded in selling fifteen million automobiles of Model T type with very little advertising. And it is a commonplace of everyone's experience that people buy automobiles primarily because the thing is in the air, because the Browns and the Smiths have an automobile — and the Browns and the Smiths are the most powerful motive force in human history. After the Brown automobile has laid Jones's trenches flat with its heavy guns, the automobile advertisement may begin to operate. Once Jones has decided to buy a car he begins to shop around in the advertisements.

Amazing force of nature, the Brown–Smiths. They are behind that mysterious rhythm of nature known as Fashion, which causes short skirts to come and go like the wind, blowing where they list.

The Browns and Smiths — that is to say, imitation — are all-powerful in the theatre. It is pretty well established by inquiry that most people go to see a show because a friend recommends it, next because of what the reviews say, and only thirdly because of the advertising.

It is the same with books. Advertising cannot make a best-seller, although advertising may "snowball" a big best-seller into a huge best-seller. Advertising can make more people want the kind of book that many people already want; but advertising does not create the want. The common history of a best-selling book which does not reveal an authentic new talent is that the author's next book does not sell so well, though it is advertised much more extensively than the first book. With the third, fourth, and succeeding books the decline may be catastrophic. The reason is that the same people who said of the first book that you must not miss it told their friends that the second book was n't nearly so good. In the ears of the man with something to sell there is no gladder sound than "word-of-mouth advertising."

The enormous popularity of the cigarette was not made by the advertiser, but by the World War. There came then other mysterious forces which set everybody to puffing at the weed, including the women. A $5,000,000 advertising appropriation may "educate" the public to a particular brand of cigarette, but one cannot be certain; and in any case the cigarette habit in itself came before.

Advertising stimulates package-food consumption; but the beginning came with the secular change in American civilization away from the kitchen; or perhaps it is a new form of the immemorial American picnicking habit. The thousands of cheap candy confections consumed by millions of Americans reflect the old quick-lunch habit, the old ten-minute railroad-buffet menagerie so sadly described by Mark Twain more than sixty years ago.

As to beauty preparations: the American people used to consume vast quantities of patent medicines when it was a pioneer people racked with malaria and indigestion and miles away from a doctor. As the country filled up and prosperity increased and houses were better heated and doctors multiplied, the patent medicine bottle began to go out and the beauty jar began to come in. Advertising certainly helped to sell bottles for internal use and is now employed to sell bottles for external use; but the basic demand came not through advertising, but from a basic need, and the change has been a social change, a mass movement.

Advertising will help to sell radios, mechanical refrigeration, vacuum cleaners; but the compulsion to buy these things comes not from the advertisers but from broad currents of change in the national life as registered primarily in the Browns and Smiths.

Always it is the basic needs of a community that determine its buying behavior; and the great bulk of advertising is concerned with basic needs. In New York is unquestionably the greatest concentration of purchasing power that the world has ever seen within anything like the same area. But in the newspaper which is far and away the most powerful advertising medium in New York the receipts from automobile and radio advertising are only one sixth of the receipts from department-store and financial advertising. Yet when the specialists complain of the coercive force of advertising they do not usually think of people being coerced into buying clothes, furniture, or a few bonds for investment.

Does it seem that the efficacy of advertising, a legitimate and useful pursuit and interest, is here being brought into question? That, of course, is not so; unless it is belittling a profession to deny it the possession of magic powers. And that is a claim which both the wise man who is out to buy advertising space and the wise man who has advertising space to sell will refuse to associate themselves with.

The advertiser is not a hypnotist, but a salesman. The advertising medium is not a siren, but a show window. In studying the advertisements, the public is really shopping around. That is actually what the woman of the house does when she goes through the department-store pages in the daily paper. The way in which these pages tell their story may unquestionably tempt Mrs. Jones to go at times a bit beyond her original budget estimate. But that happens to people who build homes, and parents who send children to college, and sometimes, it is said, even to Secretaries of the Treasury. Mrs. Jones feels after a particularly seductive statement on the department-store page that she really ought not to deny herself that ravishing pair of coonskin evening slippers with the enchanting Australian heel. But the general character of Mrs. Jones's behavior in the department-stores will be shaped by her basic requirements as by herself determined; and these requirements were determined when she met Mrs. Brown in her new spring costume and for the first time realized how shabby she, Mrs. Jones, was looking.

Let us end on a lyrico-historical note: —

What a relief it is to escape from the rush and clamor of modern American life to the peace and leisure of another uncommercialized century and another non-hustling clime! How quaintly pleasant are the street cries of old London and of old Paris about which many books have been written: the characteristic cry of the hot-muffin man, and the fried-fish man, and the old-clothes man, and the cat's-meat man, and the knife grinder and the chimney sweep! But what they all were doing, of course, in those romantic days, was advertising their goods and services. For the moment it is hard to recall just what is the peculiar sound produced by the man who drives a pair of goats down the streets of Malaga in Spain, and will milk them at your doorway into your own pail; but the yell which he emits is not essentially different in purpose and in ethical content from the sound made by Messrs. Wanamaker, Filene, Field, and Hahn in the department-store advertisements.

IV

HIS MACHINES

"And what," says Mrs. Smith, turning to her dinner guest on the right, "would you say, Mr. Jones, is the outlook for Love in the Machine Age?"

Poor Mr. Jones, thus abruptly summoned from the lady on his other side and the subject of Havana in February, does what nearly all of us do in similar crises. Hard-beset folk whom you suddenly invite to express an opinion on the place of bacon and eggs in a well-balanced diet are apt to say, "Well, eh, just what do you mean by bacon and eggs, Mrs. Smith?" Or, invited without due warning to state whether they prefer the early hours of morning in the country to the peace that comes with the sunset, they may say, "But just what do you mean by a sunset?"

So in the present case, Jones, thinking fast, says, "It depends on just what you mean by the Machine Age, Mrs. Smith."

"Why," says his hostess, and pauses just a moment to gather her ideas. She is a woman of intelligence, of wide reading and retentive memory, and given to thinking on what she has read and heard.

"The Machine Age?" she says. "Can we get away from it anywhere, Mr. Jones? In the adjacent room is the radio to which you listened only a little while ago, and you made a point of comparing the reception with the tone of our old mechanical piano for which we still have a liking, and the graphophone. In the kitchen, if you will take my word for it, we have our electropneumatic refrigerator, and the electric stove, and a variety of electric coffeepots, stewpans, chafing dishes, and toasters. Not far away is the vacuum cleaner which will pick up the bread crumbs that you are now dropping on the carpet, and near by is the laundry machine which will take care of the tablecloth on which you have let fall just a trace of the cranberry sauce; and the electric pressing irons. And of course you must not let me forget the dishwashing machine. Scattered through other rooms of our simple apartment, Mr. Jones, there must be an odd dozen of miscellaneous machines: electric curling irons, and a couple of electric pads which in certain contingencies are preferable to the old hot-water bottle, two lamps for baking my rheumatism, a clock that runs by electricity — My dear Mr. Jones, what do I mean by the Machine Age!"

Being under no compulsion, like Jones, to give

attention to a hostess and simultaneously to improvise an opinion and an attitude on Love in the Machine Age, let us snatch just half a minute to frame for ourselves a brief definition of the essential terms in the problem which Mrs. Smith has raised. It is really only one term, since a definition of Love is either unnecessary or else beyond us in the very brief time at our disposal. But what is a machine? Well, shall we say that a machine is an inanimate tool? It is a something built out of any kind of raw material other than living protoplasm, and composed of levers, wheels, pulleys, poles, aerials, wires, magnetos, fields of force, and so on. A machine has two essential traits. It is lifeless, — as when a man says indignantly, "Do you think I am a man or a machine?" — and it is a tool. A machine may have any kind of spark except the vital spark, and it must perform a useful function. As to a Machine Age, it is presumably an age which is rich in machines, or rejoices in machines, or is dominated by machines, or all three together.

Making a Noise Like a Machine

Now when Mrs. Smith speaks of Love in the Machine Age, or for that matter of almost anything else in the Machine Age, the chances are that she is thinking of the lifelessness, of the non-humanity of the machine, rather than of its instrumentalism. Her main interest is in a something that operates without consciousness, rather than in the specific nature of the operation or of the product. And what Mrs. Smith means by machines and Machine Ages, most of the books that she has read on the subject mean; and what she has overlooked or failed sufficiently to analyze, a good many books on the subject have overlooked or failed to take into account.

Thus, perhaps four fifths of Mrs. Smith's machines, reckoning by money investment and the rôle which they play in her life, are not machines at all. They are mechanical contrivances, but they are not tools. She does not use them to produce things, but only satisfactions. They are not a means to an end, but an end in themselves. They are not producers' goods, as the economists call tools and raw materials; they are consumers' goods, as the economists call things ready to be enjoyed.

Let us take another look around Mrs. Smith's apartment, and count the real machines and the things that only look like machines. You will find that the lady is not living in a Machine Age to anything like the extent she believes. The vacuum cleaner is a machine, because it is a tool for cleaning carpets; but the radio is not a machine, because it is not a tool — it is only a satisfaction, like a violin.

The washing machine is a machine, because it is a tool; but the pianola is not a machine, because it is not a tool any more than a tenor voice is a tool. The electric iron, toaster, coffeepot, and rheumatism pad are machines, because they are tools. But the graphophone is not a machine, for all its humming and buzzing and whirring; it is no more a tool than Rosa Ponselle is a tool. The electric light, summary and symbol of the Machine Age, is perhaps 10 per cent tool; the rest is joy and amusement. Yes, this electric light, shield and blazon of a mechanical civilization which pushes buttons and throws switches, is, in our homes, not a machine; it is a commodity. The telephone — what shall we say of the telephone? It is a machine for Mrs. Smith's husband down town, where he employs it as a tool in his business, as a substitute for secretaries' fingers and messengers' legs. The telephone is a machine — that is to say, a tool — in Mrs. Smith's apartment when she employs it to call up the grocer and the butcher and the doctor. But it is not a machine during half of Mrs. Smith's day, in her prolonged talks with her friends. The telephone then performs nothing useful. It is a recreation, a plaything.

After dinner Mrs. Smith is taking Mr. Jones and the others to that new Russian film in which the bourgeoisie turns out to be even worse than Mr. Stalin ever suspected. The trip is made in the two-thousand-dollar family car driven by Mr. Smith, and it lasts just long enough to permit the following observations.

Detroit and Hollywood

When people speak of the Machine Age we may take it for granted that nine times out of ten they are thinking of the automobile and the moving pictures. How can it be otherwise? The turbines which grind out kilowatts for light, heat, and power are tucked away somewhere on the edge of the city where perhaps one consumer in ten thousand sees them. The machines which make steel girders for skyscrapers are off somewhere in Pittsburgh and Birmingham, where possibly one in every ten thousand American rent payers ever sees them. The machines that make shirtings and coatings and carpetings; the machines that make breakfast food and cook meats and vegetables, and seal them into cans; the machines that weld bathtubs and paint linoleum — these machines the average man seldom sees. The famous machine known as the Railroad the average man does see and hear, even though long acquaintance has dulled him to its presence. And in the city he knows the machines of Rapid Transit which snatch him up and carry him away in a storm of speed and glare and noise and heat and utter helplessness. But even the Railroad, even the subway, hold a poor second place among the furnishing of the Machine Age. The thing that makes and marks the Machine Age is *the* Machine — the Car, the Automobile.

For three quarters of a century we had the railroad, for a century and a half the steam engine, and people were greatly concerned over the effects of machines and the future of machines. But only with the automobile did the Machine Age arrive for us, simply because it surrounded us with Machines. The automobile is in every rod of street and highway, moving, parking, congesting, flaring, backfiring, green-lighting, red-lighting, right-turning, left-turning, no-turning on red light, slaying forty thousand people a year, elbowing its way into the family budget ahead of food and drink, elbowing its way to the forefront of the conscious thought of the nation, recasting the morals of the nation, redistributing its population, reshaping its industrial structure, giving its name to an epoch, — the Age of the Automobile, — becoming for the outside world the very symbol of America: this machine called the Automobile, together with that other machine called the Movie.

Only — the automobile and the moving pictures are not machines. They are mechanical, but they are not tools. The moving picture is never a tool. The automobile is a tool when it becomes a taxi or a truck. But for the great majority of the people, and in the mass effect, it is not the taxi and the truck that count; it is the pleasure car. The automobile that dominates a nation's thoughts is not a tool, but an end in itself. It is a toy. It is the hugest, costliest, most absorbing plaything that a nation ever treated itself to. It comes in useful, of course, but it is not bought for utility. It is bought for that rare enjoyment which in history has been reserved for the privileged few — the command of speed and space. It is bought for the purpose of enabling millions of Americans to burn up expensive concrete roads with high-taxed gasoline. The American automobile is a luxury. In the sense of being a tool, a device for producing or doing something useful, the average American's automobile is no more a tool than the rich American's polo pony is a tool.

This insistence on the distinction between machines that are tools and machines that are not tools will not, I trust, impress the reader as super-refined dialectic or pedantry. To stress the fact that the automobile is most often not a tool but a plaything is not logic-chopping, since the distinction leads to a profound difference in our view of the American people to-day. It obviously is of vital importance for our picture of American civilization whether 25,000,000 automobiles mean production or consumption, mean toil or recreation, enslavement or leisure, shoulders bent under the yoke or shoulders bent over a reluctant spark plug. It is a point which we shall be compelled to take up again after a brief return to Mrs. Smith, whom we shall not even bother to remind, lest we become tedious, that the "machines" by which she finds herself surrounded in apartment and garage represent an investment of perhaps six hundred dollars in real machines and four thousand dollars in machines that are playthings, — radio, mechanical piano, graphophone, automobile, — that is to say, animate tools, not machines.

Robots

When Mrs. Smith addresses herself to Mr. Jones for a statement on Love in the Machine Age she is likely to transgress against exact thinking in more ways than one. We have seen that a machine is an inanimate tool. And we have seen that people very frequently apply the term "machine" to things that are not tools. But of greater ultimate significance is the habit of applying the term "machine" to human beings.

In speaking of Love in the Machine Age, or Parenthood or Art or Literature or Marriage in the Machine Age, Mrs. Smith, together with most of the authors she has read on the Machine Age, is apt to slide into one of those easy and frequently unperceived transitions which so utterly transform the meaning of words and of things. Mrs. Smith, quite unconscious of how it happened, finds herself no longer thinking of the Machine Age as an era in which men use a great many machines. She is thinking of it as an age in which men have themselves become machines.

When Mrs. Smith wonders if romantic love is possible in a Machine Age, she is almost asking Mr. Jones what he thinks are the chances of romantic love ever inflaming the heart of a steam shovel or a thermostat. When she speaks of Marriage in the Machine Age, she is almost thinking of the institution of wedlock as it flourishes among electric refrigerators. When she raises the question of the Family in the Machine Age, almost she is asking what form the family will assume when compressed-air hammers mate with internal-combustion engines and produce offspring in the form of, let us say, sturdy oxyacetylene torches and beautiful streamline electric bread toasters. When Mrs. Smith and her authors and most of us say Machine Age, we are most often thinking of an age out of which sentient human existence has vanished, leaving only push buttons and wheels.

This is the celebrated idea of the Robot contributed by the Bohemian dramatist Capek to the cause of loose thinking in the world. The author of *R.U.R.* did not himself think loosely. He set out to write an anti-capitalist satire. When he pictured Science inventing the all-metal Robot as an incomparably more efficient substitute for the human worker, Capek was assailing an economic system in which the individual worker, as he saw the matter, was only a tool in the hands of the employers and rulers of society. He assailed a social scheme in which individual man served his purpose best when he was completely dehumanized by being reduced to a single mechanical function. The Czech playwright indicted a particular form of economic organization which robbed the ordinary man of his human initiative, his freedom, his human worth and dignity. Perhaps it would be more correct to say that he indicted, not an economic system, but a political system. He assailed the idea of the omnipotent State which, as we see now under Communism even more than under Capitalism, dehumanizes its citizens in the interest of a final purpose, which essentially makes man into a tool for the creation of a particular product.

That cry of indignation in the Robot play was directed against the tyranny of men over men and not the tyranny of technology over men. But what most of us have done is to accept the Robot in the latter sense. We have come to feel that because of the multiplication of machines to-day men are actually turning into machines. In a Machine Age the iron is supposed to be actually entering into men's souls, turning human beings first, presumably, into semi-ferrous products, and ultimately, I suppose, into something completely metallic. Forgetting the climax of the Capek fable, which is not of men becoming iron Robots, but of the iron Robots becoming men, we find ourselves haunted by the dread of men turning into things of steel and chromium and manganese, their hearts into leather bellows, their thoughts into radio waves.

Obviously there is a very real problem in this question of Love in the Machine Age, and I am not denying that there are times when hostesses at dinner and authors at their desks grapple with that real problem. Love, marriage, and the family are bound to evolve with the evolution of machines. Love is apt to differ, though not in essentials, when the scene is a mediæval Balkan village and when it is 1931 New York. Marriage obviously is not quite the same institution when the husband drives the plough and the wife spins the flax as when the husband takes a flying machine to San Francisco on business and the wife takes the subway to her own arts and crafts studio-salesrooms near the Grand Central Terminal. The family has obviously felt the impact of the machines which bake the bread somewhere twenty-five miles away and wash the linen perhaps a hundred and fifty miles away, and so provide the wife and mother with the leisure either for studying law or for bridge.

But these changes, more or less profound, wrought by the machines in the structure of society are not the things that people have in mind when they contemplate the horrors of life in a completely mechanized America. Foreigners and native sons alike speak of that American future as of a frozen existence. The landscape of American life is a lunar one. Human machines move about the scene, but without the capacity for love or laughter, and without freedom. They are men and women in whom organs and dimensions have attained or are approaching the inorganic condition of wheels, levers, pulleys, dynamos, currents, resistances. Is a machine capable of loving? Is a machine free to love? A machine may be more powerful than an army with banners, but it is never free. A thousand horsepower is under the compulsion to punch 14,567 round holes of 2.3 millimetres in diameter through 43 inches of steel in 51 seconds. Never is it within the power of that thousand horsepower to add just one hole so as to make the number 14,568, or to make the diameter 2.3015 millimetres or the time 51½ seconds.

This is what troubles Mrs. Smith's soul when she thinks of Love in a Machine Age, and what has troubled the souls of many good men when they think of America in the Machine Age. They are all under the terror of the Robot. They see machines doing something much more than making themselves the masters of men, as indeed they sometimes become. They see machines transforming mankind into machines after their own image — which the machine never does. Because the business of wheat growing is becoming mechanized we assume that the grower and the eater of the wheat are being transformed into machines; but this is not so. Because clothes are washed by machines in the laundry we assume that the girls who manipulate them are in danger of becoming mechanized: yes, this young laundry worker on an eight-hour schedule is a Robot when compared with the pre-industrial laundress who was also the pre-industrial cook, baker, seamstress, wife, and mother, operating on a sixteen-hour schedule.

Because, in short, America is so preëminently of the Machine Age, with ever so many more machines per capita than the rest of the world, it follows that American life has already gone far toward becoming, and in time must completely become, one vast mechanical action. Life in America will become inanimate, automatic, and, what is the same as automatic, unfree. Life in America will be one vast complex of machinery punching 14,567 holes of 2.3 millimetres in diameter through 43 inches of steel in 51 seconds — never more, never less, never thinking, never feeling, never purposing, never seeking, never wearying, never experimenting, but only and eternally moving up and down, up and down; up, down; up, down; up . . .

A People That Never Stays Put

This is what is feared for America in the Machine Age; and this future is foreseen for a people that above all others denies, in its temper and its behavior, the essential definitions of the mechanical. We invoke a future of Robotism for a people essentially febrile, emotional, restless, impatient, footloose, free. We are speaking of a people that has been in motion for three hundred years and is still in motion. It is a pioneer people that continues to discover new frontiers when it has conquered the old ones. When the Pacific Ocean is reached and the free land is gone, it refuses to abide by the text-books; it finds a new frontier in the oil of Kansas-Oklahoma-Texas, and another frontier in the sunshine and movies of Hollywood, and another in the automobiles of Detroit. We are predicting mechanization and fossilization for a people that tears down its skyscrapers every fifteen years and rebuilds its towns every twenty-five years. We are speaking of a people that has developed, beyond any other, a genius for discovering and surmounting new social frontiers; so that after the conquest of the Mississippi Valley, and the Far West, and the Coast, and the Northwest, and Florida-California, and Oklahoma-Detroit, the march goes on vertically — by the millions to the high-school frontier; by the hundreds of thousands to the college frontier; to the symphony-orchestra frontier, the Tourist Third Cabin frontier. . . .

The vital point about the American and his machines escapes us. It is this: in the very intensity with which he invents machines the American asserts his unmechanical, febrile, restless, searching nature. He is always inventing in order to do things differently. Of course he wants to do things more quickly, more cheaply, more quietly, more smoothly, more elegantly, but the compelling motive is to do things differently. He is always trying to increase the 14,567 holes and the 2.3 millimetres and the 43 inches of thickness, and reduce the 51 seconds. Far from being the slave of a machine rhythm, — of the unchanging up, down; up, down; up, down, — he refuses to accept the routine oscillation; he accelerates it, he alters it, he shock-absorbs it, he gives it a six-coat finish. He is the eternal tinkerer, the engineer, the machinist, but not the machine. He is the man above all others who refuses to build his machines or his houses or his business offices for eternity, as the foolish English manufacturers do, or the Italian peasants. He builds deliberately with the design that it shall all be changed in another five, ten, twenty years.

Americans who dread the effects of the Machine Age, and Europeans who shudder over the "Americanization of Europe," are the terrorized victims of a theory. When they see on this continent the reduction of the free, spontaneous life to the clamp and vise and gear of the machine, they see things *a priori*. They see life in America becoming what the machine ought to make it. They do not stop to inquire what American life in this Machine Age has actually become. They do not ask whether America's Machine Age may not really be more spontaneous, more unpredictable, more innovating, more experimental than life in the most machineless corner of the Balkans, or south of the Yangtze River.

The Man With the Hoe

The Yangtze River! Let us turn to Mrs. Smith — by a miracle of time-space Relativity she is now back in her place at the head of her dinner table — and ask whether she would mind subjecting her guests to a simple little experiment. Would Mrs. Smith mind asking her guests each to try to think of a machine at work, — up, down; up, down; up, down, — and then state what specific picture is evoked in his or her mind? Mrs. Smith would be only too delighted to put the question, and she is sure the others would love to do their part. Thank you very much, Mrs. Smith; you are so kind.

The question is put and the answers flash up rapidly around the table. Jones says he is thinking of the Ford conveyor belt where men spend the working day and their working life giving a half-twist to bolt number 345. The lady on Jones's right says she can't help thinking of Gastonia, where young girls spend ten hours a day feeding the spindles in a daze that is surely automatic. One gentleman says he may be old-fashioned, but he still thinks of Mrs. Browning's "Do ye hear the children weeping?" His daughter, who has been on a world tour, thinks of the little girls she saw — a rather serious-minded tourist she must have been — in the cotton mills of Osaka and Shanghai and Bombay. Obviously there can be no quarreling with these answers.

But there is one guest present, — well, what is the use of beating about the bush? — the writer of these lines, as he tries to summon to his mind the perfect symbol for what is fixed, monotonous, unfree, mechanical, finds himself thinking, not of machines in factories, but of human beings in rice fields. This eternal up, down; up, down; up, down; never changing, never swerving, first this thing, then that thing, then this thing, then that thing, from day to day and year to year — what is this but the eternal peasant motion of history?

To the young girls in the Gastonia mills the factory life is, in the great majority of cases, an escape from monotony to excitement, from domestic confinement into the free life. The girl operatives in Shanghai are part of the new hope in China, and the girl mill hands of Bombay are part of the force behind Gandhi. They connote life and growth. But the bent back and bowed shoulders and slow arm swing of ten thousand years of European peasantry, the squat and crouch of twenty thousand years of Asiatic tillage — there you have the closest approach to the thing that good Mrs. Smith fears when she sees men turning into machines. Steam and electricity will never turn men into machines to the degree that 200,000,000 Chinese coolies are machines from before sunrise to long after sunset. The perfect type of the "mechanical" motion, the lifeless motion, is in the ploughman; it is he who homeward plods his weary way. From the beginning of history the lively, foot-loose, free people have been in the cities; the city mob gets its name from it mobility. The country-side produces its clodhopper. Let us not be too greatly afraid, therefore, of our machines dehumanizing mankind into their own shape. Laboring mankind is really nearest to a machine in the peasant routine, when furrow comes after furrow, and sheaf after sheaf, and chore after chore, and one day after another, and the years, and the centuries, without change and without movement — as among the people of the Yangtze and the Ganges, whom the Machine Age has not touched.

Compare with the fixity of the world's non-machined peasant masses the obvious facts of the American tempo. Febrile, impulsive, experimental, crusading, censoring, prohibiting, nullifying, bootlegging, riding the surf of fortune with a fierce zest in its crests and troughs, amending, concurring, repealing, reducing four-year terms to two-year terms, expanding two-year terms to four-year terms, electing, appointing, recalling, scaling heaven by so many ladders, by anti-trust laws, by pro-trust laws, by mayors, by city managers, by city commissions, by municipal ownership, by municipal operation, by regulation, by farm boards, by tariffs, by tariff commissions, by Greenbackism in 1874, by Bryanism in 1896, by Brookhartism in 1930 — if this is what the Machine Age has done to mechanize the American people, why is Mrs. Smith so badly worried? She thinks of the machine which punches 14,567 holes of 2.3 millimetres diameter in 51 seconds, on and on into eternity, or as long as steel and lubricant will endure, and she fears that fate for the American who never does the same thing for any length of time, whose very nature it is always to live in feast or in famine, always to do things with all his might, to hit the line hard, to do things up brown — and you never quite know where you have him. He is Puck, but Mrs. Smith and her favorite authors in sociology have got into the habit of regarding him as a Robot.

Forty years ago a non-native author saw the American in a quite different light, saw him as one who "turns a keen untroubled face home, to the instant need of things." To this foreign observer the American, far from being a machine, was a man perpetually on the alert. He is that still. He is not only essentially unmechanical in his restlessness and his foot-looseness, he is not even to be thought of as a man who is primarily absorbed by the business of the machine. Primarily his machines are playthings. This is literally true, as I hope I have shown, of so many of his machines which are designedly toys — his automobiles, radios, films, graphophones, airplanes, and soon television, no doubt. But it is true even of the American's approach to the machines that are unmistakably tools — his power hammers and cranes and conveyors and giant shears and drills. Their primary appeal to him is not as tools but as novelties, as ends in themselves. They are esteemed greatly for the greater quantities of goods they can produce and the greater sums of money they can make, but more they are esteemed because they are a newer, cleverer way of doing things. They are different.

The Happy Child

The next time you see a male American in the barber's chair, having the back of his neck clipped by electric scissors, the scanty fuzz on the top of his head massaged by an electric vibrator, the stray hairs on his white sheet of penance sucked up by a miniature vacuum machine, the hot towel for his face cooking in a bright nickel electric oven, the skin on his face bathed by a violet-ray machine, the polish on his shoes dried by an electric drier — when you see all these things don't feel too unhappy and say, "Here is a man fast on the way toward being himself transformed into a machine." He is not. He is not even a man primarily concerned with a better way of having his hair trimmed, his towel boiled, his shoes dried, his trousers brushed. Essentially he is a child taking delight in the hum and buzz and glint and click of a lot of electric toys. He adores playing with them, and to save his self-respect and ward off comment he finds some use for them and calls them machines. But what he loves is not the use, but the buzz.

V

HIS MOTHER AND HIS WIFE

For the perfect example of what the Machine Age has done to the soul of America, for the climax and triumph of Standardization, it has been suggested that we cannot do better than turn to the Western Union Telegraph Company and its competitors. The wire companies have laid a heavy hand on the nation's finer feelings. This they have done by compiling a large stock of form messages which permit the customer to express himself on every conceivable human occasion with complete adequacy and without the slightest mental effort. If Jones, for instance, happens to think of his old mother on Mother's Day, all he needs to do —

Why, no! Jones does not even have to recall that this is Mother's Day. Western Union and Postal Telegraph have been reminding him these last several days, in large display advertisements in the newspapers, of the approach of Mother's Day. Their efforts have been bravely seconded by the florists, who have stumbled upon the happy thought that flowers are an excellent medium for expressing one's love for one's mother. All that Jones needs to do, then, is to call up the telegraph company and leave an order for the dispatch, early on Mother's Day, of Form No. 18. He may then walk over to the barber shop to have his hair cut, while Western Postal sends humming over the wires to the gray-haired little woman in the old homestead the pulsating message: "Mother of Mine, I have many blessings for which to be thankful, but the greatest of these is you, and my thoughts are with you this Mother's Day." So daughter at college, as of the less sentimental sex and the more economical, calls up the Union Telegraph and asks for No 89: "To-day I salute the most precious of all people — my mother."

For every occasion, for every anniversary, for every festivity, for every fatality, the telegraph company has seen to it that the American of the year 1931 shall be spared the pains of composing anywhere from ten to fifty words. While the barber cuts Jones's hair and the manicure girl polishes his nails and the bootblack shines his shoes, the Radio Corporation of America is voicing for him his affection, his love, his sympathy, his pride, his congratulations, his regrets, his condolences. According to directions, Commercial Cables is gay for him, grave for him, sentimental for him, tearful or boisterously good-fellow. That is the Machine Age of it. And the Standardization would be, of course, the fact that at any one moment a hundred identical messages of love, affection, grief, and sympathy are coursing through the American atmosphere from Maine to Florida and from Los Angeles to Seattle.

It is a pitiful and portentous spectacle. One need hardly ask what it bodes for the spiritual and intellectual integrity of a nation, this substitution of canned heart throbs for fresh, this expenditure on the old mother at home of telephone and telegraph tolls in lieu of a few minutes with paper and pen and a touch of real affection. But before we have definitely identified in this new American custom another factor contributing to the atrophy of men's souls and the triumph of machines, it may be in order to ask a question.

Mr. Owen D. Young's Predecessors

Have you ever read J. M. Barrie's *Sentimental Tommy*? If you are in years more than fifty, you probably know the book, and perhaps you may remember that one form in which young Tommy's exceptional literary gifts found expression was in writing letters for the villagers. At the age of fourteen, let us say, Tommy was an excellent hand at love letters. He would write — But it may very well be that you are in years under forty. You are not acquainted with Barrie's story, but you have read, of course, nearly everything by Chekhov. In that case you may have read the little story called "At Christmas Time." The old peasant woman, Vasilisa, and her husband, Peter, have just hired the services of the village scribe, Yegor. The letter is to their daughter, who married and went away to the city four years ago and, after writing to them twice, has not been heard from.

"What am I to write?" Yegor asked again.

"What?" asked Vasilisa, looking at him angrily and suspiciously. "You are not writing for nothing; no fear, you'll be paid for it. Come, write: 'To our dear son-in-law, Andrey Hrisanfitch, and to our only beloved daughter, Yefimya Petrovna, with our love we send a low bow and our parental blessing abiding forever.'"

"Written; fire away."

"'And we wish them a happy Christmas; we are alive and well, and I wish you the same, please the Lord . . . the Heavenly King.'"

Vasilisa pondered and exchanged glances with the old man.

"And I wish you the same, please the Lord . . . the Heavenly King," she repeated, beginning to cry.

She could say nothing more. And yet before, when she lay awake thinking at night, it had seemed to her that she could not get all she had to say into a dozen letters.

Or if not Chekhov, you are sure to have read during these last few years a good many books about the way of life among peoples who have not been altogether spoiled by the Industrial Revolution and by literacy. In such studies of pre-industrial man you are sure to have come across the universal figure of the village letter writer. He flourishes in China and Japan and India, as in Russia, and Italy, and Ireland. He squats in the bazaar, in the public square, in his own cabin, and to him come Nipponese mothers for letters to their sons with the army in Manchuria, and Calabrian wives for letters to their husbands in Buenos Aires, and Connaught girls for messages to their sweethearts on the Boston police force. And everywhere, in Yokohama, in Cittanova, in Roscommon, these simple souls find it easy enough to pour out their hearts to the letter writers, but stand tongue-tied in awe before the specific demand of the blank page. The professional scribe thereupon writes as he pleases. He knows what mothers should say to their sons and wives to their husbands. Being seventy and toothless, he knows what girls want to say to their sweethearts. And his message, in style and detail, is quite as far removed from the original source as Western Postal's Form 55 on Mother's Day. Messrs. Newcomb Carlton and Clarence Mackay are only pepetuating an ancient Folkway.

Of course there is an objection to be noted. This peasant mother in Chekhov and this Hindu girl in the Bengal village are at the mercy of the professional letter writer's formulas because they are, as a matter of fact, illiterate. But the American patrons of Forms 55 and 74 have all of them been to school, a great many of them to high school, many of them to college. They know how to write. Why don't they?

But don't they write? And do they know how? A great many sons still write to their mothers on Mother's Day or mother's birthday — many more, I will venture to say, than send form telegrams. By no means all the girls at college are in too great a hurry for a date to do more for father's birthday than wire him Form 74, "Daddy Dear." They write a letter and send him a book, and they have the book charged to him.

For it is with this subject of the people and civilization of the United States as it used to be generally with the subject of Woman, and still is in considerable measure: one fact makes a generalization, and three instances make a universal truth. At all times it has been the rule that if a man at lunch is observed putting red pepper into his coffee the incident will be reported in the following words: "There are some men who have a queer habit of putting red pepper into their coffee." But if the coffee drinker should be female, the circumstance invariably gives rise to the statement: "Woman has the extraordinary habit of putting red pepper into her coffee. Some authorities attribute this to her historic subordination to masculine rule; other authorities are inclined to explain red pepper in coffee as a secondary sex characteristic."

So it is with ever so many traits of American civilization as depicted by foreign observers and native sons. Fifty Americans wire on Mother's Day. Five thousand Americans write letters on Mother's Day. Ergo: "In nothing, perhaps, does American standardization manifest itself as in the habit of sending stereotyped telegraphic messages on Mother's Day."

The Higher Literacy

And do all Americans know how to write because they have been to school? It is, of course, a rash conclusion. Even among educated people there is only a small minority to whom the business of writing is not a task. Literate man in the mass exhibits in the presence of pen and paper the same timidity that possessed poor Vasilisa in the presence of the village letter writer. The gift of expression is far less common than the gift of self-expression. See what a boast the English people make of the tongue-tied shyness of the English, as when the son goes off to war and father and son cannot bring themselves to speak out their heartache. So perhaps the Western Postal form messages are a part of an Anglo-Saxon tradition of emotional reticence; and it should be to the credit of the Radio Corporation that its stencils permit parents and children to express a love that would else go silent and for naught.

The notion that sincere feeling cannot be expressed in a formula is absurd. It has been the questionable good fortune of most of us to read in the newspapers the letters written by infatuated old fools to slim young sirens and by women of years to young men. Such documents are always turning up in breach of promise suits and in the domestic relations courts. They show that elderly men and women of fair literacy, when caught on the swell of a real passion, almost invariably resort to a vocabulary of roses and stars, and limpid eyes mirroring Heaven, and lips whispering messages from the isles of bliss; he is her Laddie-Boy aged sixty-five, and she is his Dream Girl in the early fifties. The poetic quotations in such legal proceedings are nearly always from "The Road to Mandalay," "A Fool There Was," and "Dan McGrew." It is a fact of newspaper record that men and women beset by love will go down to destruction shouting the most dreadful banalities.

Fifty years before Americans were standardized into telegraphic form messages, people wrote letters to each other out of the *Complete Letter Writer,* containing one hundred specimens for every possible occasion. One hundred and fifty years ago, little boys writing to their mothers from school addressed them as Honoured Parent, the whole letter dictated by the headmaster. And thirty-five hundred years ago, as we have seen, the Egyptian mother told the village writer that she wished to write to her son in garrison at Jerusalem, and the scribe wrote what he thought was suitable to the occasion. The form of the message does not exclude a living heart behind it.

Mother Worship

The mother cult in the United States, as part of the all-pervading woman worship which was long ago identified as a basic American trait, needs the caustic and corrective examination to which it has been subjected by the lighter satirists. This religious code maintains that every prize fighter goes into the ring thinking only of the little woman and the kiddies. Every bacteriologist glues his eye to the microscope through the weary years for the sake only of the little woman and the kiddies. Every aviator is out to break the 42,187-feet altitude record for the sake of the wife and the kiddies. Unmarried prize fighters, bacteriologists, and aviators are spurred on to effort and victory by the thought of the old mother back there in the little whitewashed cottage. If the Nobel prize-winning bacteriologist forgets to mention his old mother, the reception committee in the old home town will remember her. If the reception committee should happen to forget, the committee's publicity agent will remember her. If the publicity agent should forget, the reporters will remind him of his mother. The hint has not been wanting in the press that Professor Einstein discovered Relativity for the sake chiefly of his women folks.

Given these amiable lunacies in gyneolatry, there can be no quarrel with the newspaper humorist for suggesting that the cult of Mother's Day may have profited by the activities of the American florist; just as Father's Day is not altogether frowned upon by the necktie manufacturers; just as Apple Week is said to find some support among the apple growers of the Pacific Northwest Coast; just as Fire Prevention Week is said to encounter no undue hostility from the sprinkler and chemical manufacturers; just as Old Home Week finds no irreconcilable enemies among the railroad companies and the bus lines. The newspaper paragrapher is obviously useful as well as amusing when he makes his thrust at this particular bit of nonsense, and goes his way.

Harder to accept is the humorless satirist and sociologist who picks up the mother jest and turns it into a jeremiad, who picks up a grain of incongruity and magnifies it into a problem and a menace. With a mighty clanking of scientific apparatus and at enormous length, people fell to work soon after the Armistice to expose the infantilism which inheres in the Mother's Day cult, and the arrested development, and the narcissism, and other defects and aberrations peculiar to the American people. Sometimes, to be sure, the touch faltered a bit; as when the analyst seemed to find it hard to decide just which was responsible for Mother's Day, the essentially adolescent nature of the Americans or the Western Union Telegraph Company and the Associated Florists. The dilemma was surmounted, of course, by deciding that Mother's Day was the result of the telegraph company and the florists bringing their full power to bear upon the adolescent instincts of the American people.

That the mother cult in America should be compared with the Frenchman's worship of his *maman* is obviously too much to ask. It is too much to ask of a social critic busy with the abnormalities of the American scene that he take a look at other civilizations.

That the mother cult in the United States should be studied in the light of the primitive matriarchal institutions of the Protochukchis is too much to ask. In comparing Jones with the primitives it is the rule to cite from primitive civilization only the evidence that will count against Jones, and never for him.

But it is not too much to ask that students of Mother's Day in America, and of the broader subject of woman worship in America, should occasionally give a thought to the possibility that the cult may be not altogether an aberration, or at least something more than an aberration. Merely in idle curiosity, merely to take his mind off really serious questions, merely for a change, the observer of Mother's Day might say: "I wonder if there isn't something in American history and American statistics that will explain, to some extent, why Americans make so much more fuss about their mothers than other nations do?"

Such a question, candidly put and pondered, might ultimately direct the inquirer's attention to the fact that in the United States — even in the United States of super-booming 1928 prosperity — nine housewives out of ten do their own housework.

This interesting fact leads us to what I think is the just inference that in the average articulate American family the children spend much more time in close communion with their mothers than in the average articulate European family.

They Do Their Own Work

By the articulate classes I mean those that give form and stamp to the national life. They are the classes that count, the classes one has in mind when one says that Englishmen do this or Americans do that. In this sense, even in the most advanced countries of Europe the peasant population and the industrial masses are not articulate. Even in England, where the working classes have become definitely articulate in the political life, they are still but a timid voice in the rounded national chorus. When you speak of what books and newspapers Englishmen read and what music the Germans listen to, you mean perhaps 10 per cent of the English or the German people. But when you speak of what Americans read or play or telegraph to their mothers, you are thinking of a potential 75 per cent of the American people. Whatever may be America's "contribution" to history, the number of participants in that contribution is easily five times as great as in England or Germany. The people who count are five times as many here as in other countries.

The case might be stated in terms of family income. Take ten English families having an annual income of $2500; eight out of the ten families almost certainly keep a servant. Take ten American families with the same income; one out of the ten will keep a servant. One element in European life that never fails to surprise the visiting American is the presence of domestic servants in "poor" homes. One thing that never fails to astonish Europeans is the number of "rich" American women who do their own housework. The wife of the English university professor will stint herself on clothes, on food, on coal, but there will nearly always be a couple of sturdy Devon lasses to do the work of the house. The American professor's wife, herself a college graduate often, does her own cooking and cleaning, and sometimes her own washing of clothes.

Among other things she gives personal care to

her children. She performs for her children of the pre-school age the services which the English-woman or German lady of her income status delegates to the celebrated Nanny of the London *Times* classified advertisements, to the nurse, the nursery governess, and, in humbler homes, to the stout maid of all work. The wives of American clergymen with an income of $2500, or country lawyers, doctors, small merchants, college professors, bathe their own children until these can look after themselves, put them to bed, read to them. The English or German boy wheedles kitchen gratuities from "Cook," the American boy does it from his mother, for it is she who does the cooking while keeping an eye on the small children.

It is scarcely necessary to go on with the details in order to demonstrate the simple truth that the American child sees a great deal more of his mother than his European coeval of the same articulate class. It is so in the early formative years, and is emphasized in later years. The eight-year-old son of the English small-town banker is sent away from home to school. The banker's son in small-town Ohio, California, and Maine does not leave home until he goes away to college.

If, then, a member of the British House of Commons — excluding the Labor Party — is likely between the ages of six months and seventeen years to have seen his mother only one third as often as our average member of Congress has seen his, is there not some *prima facie* reason why "Mother" should bulk larger in the daily American vernacular than in the English? Whether or not the thing is desirable is quite another matter. I understand that mother fixations are dangerous things. But if the mother fixations are there, it follows that Mother's Day cannot be wholly explained as propaganda by the Associated Florists; just as Father's Day is not 100 per cent the handiwork of the necktie manufacturers. Notorious for generations has been the American habit of parents deferring to children, instead of having children defer to their elders as they do everywhere else in the world. Foreigners assert that in this country the family is dominated by the claims of the child. But if it is true that the American child is outrageously indulged and spoiled, is there not the likelihood that the child will remember with some tenderness the mother who spoiled him?

These are obvious matters, but perhaps not out of place in an inquiry dedicated to the great many obvious facts of American life which the critical temper of recent years has so amazingly succeeded in overlooking. The mother cult in America is not all ballyhoo and propaganda, because the general cult of woman in America is not all ballyhoo and propaganda. The American boy is brought up by women as European boys of equal economic and social station are not. The case of the mother and her boy up to the age of six we have seen. After six the American boy goes off to school to a woman teacher, but the European boy has a man schoolmaster. Out of every five teachers whom the American boy has met up to college age, four have been women. It is a big subject that has been much discussed, and here calls only for mention.

Implicit in the Statistics

This American respect for Womanhood, as the orator calls it, this American habit of putting woman on a pedestal, as the cooler heads call it, argues neither virtue nor demerit in the American. The tradition has a sound social-economic basis, and is due, I assume, to pioneer conditions. It is a commonplace among the statisticians that in the older countries of Europe there are more women than men, and in new countries — the United States, Australia — there are more men than women. We have to-day probably two million more males than females. England has two million more females than males, and the war is not entirely responsible. There was a large female surplus in Great Britain and Germany before the war, and a large female deficit in this country. For sixty years it has been true with us that for every one hundred women there have been nearly one hundred and five men.

American respect for womankind would thus appear to be grounded in the scarcity value of women in this country. For this reason, among others, the American male needs comparatively little encouragement from his florist and his telegraph company in order to be kind to his womenfolk. This kindness is inbred in him. The infection is in the air. It seizes upon the immigrant from Central Europe at Quarantine, and impels the peasant woman to step into her higher status as a matter of course and her menfolk to concede it as a matter of course. Countless observers, foreign and domestic, have pointed out that American men in respect to their women are like Matthew Bagnet —

Safety first in the face of new reading habits! Let it be said for the benefit of all readers under fifty that there is a book called *Bleak House* by a man named Charles Dickens. Not the least attractive group of characters in that book consists of Matthew Bagnet, ex-artilleryman with a record of service in British garrisons all around the world; his strong, brave, hard-working, cheerful wife, Mrs. Bagnet, affectionately referred to as the Old Girl; their two charming daughters, Malta and Quebec, and their son young Woolwich. Now to Matthew Bagnet has been denied the gift of ready expression. When approached on any subject, — as, let us say in modern terms, whether the family should move out to the suburbs, or whether the son should go in for aviation engineering, or whether Picasso marks an advance over Cézanne, — this Matthew Bagnet invariably turns to the Old Girl and says, "You tell them what I think." And the Old Girl tells them, with vigor and common sense and fondness for her own men.

The men of America as yet depend on their Old Girls to attend to most of the expression and self-expression for them, with one important difference. Although Matthew Bagnet respects his wife enormously, and insists he never saw the Old Girl's equal, he never owns to it before her. "Discipline must be maintained." The American male would n't dream of applying discipline to his womenfolk. He delights in telling the Old Girl what he thinks of her. He says it with flowers, with telegrams, with candy. Perhaps he gets a reminder from the Western Postal and other advertisers. But the urge is his own.

Let the critics of American gyneolatry and of its devastating effects on American civilization be patient. As the country fills up, as we cut down the male surplus and ultimately develop a female surplus, our traditional respect for women will approximate the established forms in the older countries. With that will come a weakening of the mother cult as part of our general cult of women. As America grows still richer and more urbanized and more specialized, American children will begin to see less and less of their mothers and more and more of cooks and governesses. They will see less and less of female school-teachers. Our wealthy classes have already mastered the art of sending the small boy away to what the English call a public school and we call a private school, with men teachers predominant. For the great mass of our population there are the public schools (in the American sense). In growing variety and number they are stepping in between mother and child. Below the primary grades are the kindergarten classes, the pre-kindergarten classes, the pre-school nursery, moving steadily down, one is almost tempted to say, to the pre-natal school.

VI

HIS GAMES

WE have seen in another chapter how the critical temper, as a result of delving too deep into the glands and the Unconscious, or looking too far away to the primitive and uninhibited, or looking too high up into the clouds of Utopia, may end by failing to appraise correctly so familiar an object as a two-cent morning newspaper. It is now our privilege to see very nearly the same causes operating to produce very nearly the same effect in the case of another phase of American life, almost as mysterious and baffling as a daily newspaper — and that is a baseball game.

Looking out of the window one day in quest of something in the national scheme of things that is sadly different from what it ought to be . . .

You remember, of course, the lady who sent out the maid to see what little Walter was doing and to tell him not to do it. . . .

Looking out of the window in quest of another

instance of the stupid, perverse, and generally mis-
directed behavior of the American common man,
the critical mind observes the American populace
engaged in play. People are playing harder than
any nation has ever played before, in larger numbers,
and at incomparably greater expense. Never have
there been such vast human aggregations as that
searching gaze out of the window reveals. These
armies of recreation outnumber by several times any
army ever brought on a battlefield within the same
area. On the beach at Coney Island on a midsum-
mer Sunday there may be nearly as many people as
there were Allies or Germans in the battle of the
Marne; and Coney Island is only one of a possible
hundred beaches. On a crisp November day in the
Yale Bowl there are more people than followed God-
frey de Bouillon to the Holy Land. For the country as a whole on any fine summer Sunday the
holiday makers might be equal to half the population of the Roman Empire at its height, and
their disbursements on a single day's fun would
be more than the annual revenues of the Roman
Empire.

Here, then, you would say, the critical temper
can find nothing to cavil at. In this heartening
spectacle of great masses of men on holiday, forgetting business, forgetting inhibitions, forgetting

themselves, what is there to view with alarm, or even with disapproval?

But this is to underestimate the persistence and resourcefulness of the deflating, revaluating mind. It looks out of the window, it looks up at the ceiling, it glances through the papers, it ponders a bit, and it emerges triumphant with the necessary flaming, blasting formula in just one word: —

"Vicarious."

Why, of course, how simple, when one comes to think of it! You ask what is the trouble with these great crowds which seem to be having such a good time? We will tell you, friend. It is wrong, wrong, all wrong; these people are playing Vicariously. You might as well face the dreadful truth that the overwhelming majority of our people do not really play; they only watch a few others play. They do not take part in games. They are spectators.

Colleges and Questionnaires

A word of explanation is called for. It is not my intention to suggest that the critical temper has picked up this Vicarious Hypothesis of American play out of the thin air, out of the inner consciousness, out of the whole cloth. That is not my argument. For that matter, nowhere in these chapters, dealing with what may be called the vision defects of the critical mind, is it my purpose to suggest that the critic's conclusions are without their kernel of fact. The factual nucleus is there as a rule, but overlaid and rendered unrecognizable by formula.

In the case of our reprehensible vicarious play methods the factual nub is supplied, of course, by conditions in the colleges. Popular criticism, as well as critical criticism, is seriously concerned with this evil of a few star athletes on the teams and the rest of the undergraduate body in the cheering section. It is a problem intrinsically of far greater importance than the so-called commercialization of college athletics by million-dollar stadiums and quarter-million-dollar "gates." Until we succeed in substituting for super-athletes plus snake dances a healthy system of intramural sports and competitions, it will remain true that too many American undergraduates play vicariously with their lungs and throats, instead of playing directly with their arms and legs.

Even here, to be sure, we might pause long enough to inquire whether the dimensions of the problem are really as formidable as set down in the war *communiqués*. When we speak of four dozen undergraduates in football togs and blankets on the field, and four thousand to forty thousand undergraduates in the stands, we are describing a situation that holds true for only one afternoon in the week. At other times these vicarious spectators of the football game are participants in games and recreations of their own. Day by day in the colleges there is really a great deal more non-vicarious tennis, golf, swimming, walking, climbing, running, gymnastics, skiing, skating, than the public is likely to recall in the ardor of debate; but let that pass. What matters is that the native genius for seizing upon a fact or a theory and going the limit with it, and beyond, has come to the fore. Inevitably that vicarious play in the colleges was seized upon and expanded to the dimensions of a national problem. People began to look for the vicarious symptoms on every playing field in the country, and, seeking, found them.

Inevitably there came on the scene of inquiry our good old friend, the Questionnaire. It appears that somewhere in the Middle West several thousand school children were asked to set down their favorite recreations in the order of preference. Seven thousand children between the ages of eight and twelve gave first place to the Comic Strip and second place to Reading; both of them sedentary recreations. In other words, American children do not play in any real sense. The Huck Finn and Tom Sawyer appetite is extinct. American children to-day prefer to

sit in a chair and follow the adventures of the Kat-
zenjammer Kids and the Airplane Boys in Borneo.
Under the circumstances it is little cause for wonder
that our social students have been seeking an answer
to the problem of how to save American childhood
from the blight of vicariousness.

The critical temper in America is at one with the
American questionnaire in preferring the results of
"research" to the findings of everyday experience, observation, and common sense. The analysis of seven
thousand replies in a Mid–Western questionnaire is
deemed enough to sustain the doctrine that American children do more reading of funny sheets than
they do of running, swimming, one old cat, prisoner's
base, baseball, bicycling, tree climbing. The critical
mind is always being alarmed by grave situations revealed in questionnaires because the critical mind
always looks at the questionnaire and never out of
the window at the gang playing shinny on the
asphalt. And so, by sufficient brooding over the
questionnaires, and sufficient abstention from looking
out of the window, and sufficient yielding to the
charms of the blessed word "vicarious," the case
against the American people at play assumes its
proper, that is to say, its alarming, dimensions. It
may be summed up as follows: —

Consider, on the one hand, this little band of

Walarumbas in their jungle retreat. They are lying about under the trees doing nothing. Suddenly one of them leaps to his feet, smites his hands together, and begins to dance to his own song and accompaniment. The infection spreads. In a little while that jungle glade is the scene of a leaping, dancing, chanting, improvising, sweating group of Walarumbas expressing their joy of life in spontaneous physical activity. It ends in twenty Walarumbas sinking exhausted to the ground. They have finished their game. That is Play.

Consider, on the other hand, any night in the United States. Thirty million people turn the knob of six million radios and listen to somebody. Then they turn the knob again and listen to somebody else. Then they turn off the machine and go to bed. They have sought recreation in hearing somebody else play something and sing something. They have done nothing themselves. They have played vicariously. They have exhibited not a trace of the Walarumbas playing in the jungle, either in respect to spontaneity or in respect to physical participation. America as a nation of spectators is attested by the number of paid annual admissions at professional baseball games, football games, boxing matches, racing, golf, tennis, field sports. Such annual patrons have been estimated to run as high as 75,000,000.

Non-Vicarious Statistics

Fascinated, if profoundly depressed, by these 75,-000,000 vicarious play boys in the United States every year, the critical temper as a rule omits to ask itself how big is the United States and how long is a year. Now it is reported on good authority that there are in the country 122,000,000 people, of whom about two thirds or, say, 80,000,000, are of baseball and football and boxing-match attendance age. Cut this number in half, because few women go to base-ball games and prize fights, and remember that women do go in great numbers to football games, horse races, and tennis and golf matches, and you have 50,000,000 people in the United States in the paid-admission class. But if the total number of admissions, as estimated above, is 75,000,000, it ap-pears that the average American vicarious player actually plays the part of spectator one and a half times in the course of a year, three times in the course of every two years, six times in the course of a Presidential administration.

May we assume that the average American over the age of fifteen in the course of Mr. Hoover's ad-ministration will have spent as much as six after-noons in some form of active exercise or play, as participant and not as spectator? Is it conceivable that in the course of four years he will have played six games of amateur baseball, or six rounds of golf, or spent six afternoons in swimming, or in tennis, or even have taken six long walks? If we may so reason, then it is already apparent that the American play boy is only 50 per cent vicarious and spectator. But it is permissible to ask for more than six active games in four years. Thus: —

Several million people in the country play golf. If you assume an average of five afternoons a season, golf alone will account for one quarter as many active men-days in the course of a year as all the 75,000,000 vicarious admissions at every form of sport.

Many millions of people go to the beaches in summer. On a certain Sunday in July 1930 in New York City the attendance at the Giants baseball game was 30,000, and at the Brooklyn Robins game was 18,000. But the number of people on the beach at Coney Island and the Rockaways was a million. That Sunday in Greater New York twenty times as many people were playing actively in the water or near it as were sitting vicariously in the baseball parks. You might say indeed that the nation's beaches, lakes, streams, pools, — just the water sports, — in the course of a summer will easily equal the number of paid admissions for the whole year.

Take tennis. Our college and high-school population alone is 5,000,000. Boys and girls, shall we assume that they average three afternoons a year at the game? That will give you 15,000,000 men-afternoons in tennis.

Take one sport which goes so far back to the primitive that it is truly astonishing it should escape the attention of the eye with a passion for the primitive — take the pursuit of wild game. In 1927 there were issued in the United States more than 6,000,000 hunting licenses. Say that each license represented three days in the woods with a gun, each day of eight hours, as it is likely to be in the woods. This means 144,000,000 active men-hours. Now take your 40,-000,000 baseball spectators, sitting an average of two hours on a hard bench. That means 80,000,000 men-hours. Shooting and hunting, which bulk so little in the public eye and in the sporting pages, actually come close to consuming twice as much time in America as all the professional baseball in the country. Then take fishing with its scores of millions of men-days.

Take, to unmask my batteries at last, dancing. Here is play in the perfect form. Dancing is precisely what those admirable Walarumbas do in the jungle. But it is also an occupation which has helped to designate our times. It is a dance-mad age, an age of Dancing Mothers, an age that dances while civilization is burning. How many people dance in the United States? Well, there is one approach to an estimate. Those 30,000,000 nightly radio listeners whom one writer cites as an example of American vicarious play are not all listeners. A great many radios are chiefly engaged in receiving jazz to which multitudes of young people are dancing. How many? Shall we say that 45,000,000 Americans between the ages of twenty and forty-four average ten hours of dancing a year? That would mean several times the total men-hours represented by the 75,000,000 vicarious admissions.

Take — oddly enough — baseball. You fix your mind on an average quarter-million people who daily sit in the professional baseball parks. You overlook the millions of young men who play baseball on the corner lots, in factory yards — yes, and on the asphalt pavements under the most discouraging circumstances.

This list might be continued for some time with appreciable results. But already it is apparent that active play and recreation in the United States is in overwhelming preponderance over the vicarious recreations. One item, however, demands attention, for the simple reason that it is the principal item in the play record of the American people. Yes, you have guessed it — it is the automobile.

The Great Gasoline Game

What would a conscientious and normally intelligent reporter from Mars wire home about the American automobile? He would say that never in the history of the world has there been even the semblance of approach to this spectacle of a nation going mad over a plaything. Twenty-five million pleasure cars and nearly 35,000,000 drivers mean a whole nation on wheels. It is a nation so possessed with the passion for momentum and speed that it goes dashing up and down the perfect roads without taking time to think of where it is going or why. It is a nation that seems to have been injected with a new dosage of the gypsy blood, so that great numbers of Americans do nothing but travel back and forth between tourists' camps. Americans, the man from Mars will wire home, still work hard, though not so hard as they used to; but the energy with which they play is simply astounding. He will make a calculation. Twenty million pleasure cars averaging two hours a week mean two billion auto-hours a year.

And if this reporter from the outer spaces had a streak of philosophic comment in him — a crime which the American reporter would die rather than confess — he might go on to say a word or two about the peculiar quality of the play which the American people derives from the automobile. He would point out that the entire population of a country is enjoying itself in a manner that hitherto has been the prerogative of the rulers of earth. Man has regularly established a sense of superiority over his fellow men by looking down on them from the back of a horse, or by moving swiftly among them on horseback. Aristocracy has always been rich in horse sense, if I may be permitted the word: *chevalier, cavaliere, caballero, Ritter,* the Roman equestrian, the Greek *hippeus.* The names testify to this happy privilege of looking down on pedestrians, of moving swiftly over large distances, of using and controlling a living force — in this case the steed. A horseman might, by extraordinary efforts, cover one hundred and fifty miles in a day's riding. That made him a demigod in the eyes of the clodhopper confined within a horizon measured by his legs.

This play of kings and princes is now being practised in America by very nearly the entire population of 122,000,000. The automobile driver controls not one horsepower but anywhere from twenty-five to two hundred and fifty horsepower, and he can cover, if need be, close to a thousand miles in the space of twenty-four hours. Compared with the common man of the pre-automobile age the plain

American in his car is a great deal more than a knight on his charger. He is an eagle in the air.

Does the thought of the automobile as a plaything cast a cheerier light on the subject of Americans and how vicariously they play? Not noticeably. Most statements of vicarious depression omit the automobile. The conscientious student of the subject does take notice of the automobile, but he, too, finds an ingenious way out. By taking sufficient thought it may be discovered that running about in a car is not really play. The automobile is a machine, and playing with a machine falls far short of the ideal. For that matter, by the rigid test of spontaneity and creative impulse in play, it is not real play to be playing with a bat, a golf club, a tennis racket. These are tools, that is to say, machines, that is to say, objects to be frowned upon; unless indeed one has had the happy inspiration to cut himself a baseball bat and a golf stick out of the nearest convenient tree, or has fashioned himself his own tennis racket after, presumably, killing and eviscerating his own cat. In this manner virtually all the tools which we employ in sport become machines. As for the radio jazz music to which millions dance every night, is n't it plain that its tum-tum-tum monotone is mechanical, and of the Machine, and therefore non-spontaneous? You are tempted to say, in the face of this summary disposal of the agenda of American sport, that the American people is simply out of luck. It cannot do anything right. Even when it dances to the drum beat of the jungle, which ought to be as far away from the Machine as one can imagine, it is not the real thing.

The critical mind, operating on the play habits of a nation, thus shows the same factors at work that we have observed in the case of other habits and institutions of this nation. For three reasons there is very little to be said in praise of popular play methods in the United States. (1) They are the methods employed by the great majority of the people, and therefore automatically suspect. (2) They are methods and forms of play which are not my methods and forms, I being the few of us endowed with the critical temper, and therefore automatically suspect. (3) They are play methods far removed from those of the primitive Walarumbas, and therefore automatically suspect.

1. Millions of plain people, especially in the towns where play facilities are more limited than in the open country, like to take in an occasional baseball game. Millions of young people, not so plain but still recognizably simple, love to attend football games. Other crowds love to see boxers in a ring, oarsmen in a shell, tennis players on a court. There-

fore, almost by definition, there must be something wrong with this practice of attendance at games. *Vox populi, vox absurda,* don't you know?

2. What do I, of the critical temper, consider the ideal play forms and recreation forms for the American people? Well, I think it is real fun to have a little place out in Connecticut, and to run out week-ends, and walk about in an old pair of trousers and a blue shirt, and chop down a tree occasionally, or perhaps build up the stone fences, or even go in for a little amateur carpentry on a simple one-story guest house with a big fireplace for week-end visitors, to which one can retreat one's self with a typewriter when there are too many visitors. And occasionally one goes out on a long tramp through the hills with a knapsack.

To this undeniably alluring form of play, there is but one objection. It ignores the fact that 95 per cent of the American people are not in a position, for many reasons, to buy themselves a little place in Connecticut where they may combine, in the style of the late W. E. Gladstone, the healthful exercise of tree chopping with pottering on a new translation of Homer, or some other form of typewriter exercise. Americans at play, as in so many other interests, alas, insist on being not I but themselves, living their own lives under their own economic conditions.

Jungle Rotarians

3. And the Walarumbas, who do play so spontaneously in the jungle, who do dance to music of their own impromptu choruses, who make no use of automobiles or radios or machine-turned baseball bats, golf clubs, and tennis rackets — is there any hope at all of recapturing something of that fine Walarumba play frenzy for our industrial and machine-ridden people? Well, on the subject of play among the Walarumbas, there is one thing that may be said, or at least that will here be said. It is this: There is good ground for suspecting that the critical temper misunderstands play in the jungle almost as badly as it misunderstands play in the United States.

What is the consensus of opinion among anthropologists about the freedom and spontaneity of the primitive life? Certainly the great body of scholarly opinion maintains that in the primitive society there is little freedom and little spontaneity. On every side the savage is encompassed by his taboos, affirmative and negative. He lives under a code of prescriptions and forms that apply even to his amusements. Or perhaps one had better say that many of the primitive exercises which we take to be amusements are not amusements at all. Out of the very considerable amount of leaping and chanting that punctuates the primitive routine, by no means all the leaping and chanting is spontaneous or individualistic — or play.

Take this institution of the Primitive Dance, which has become the symbol of primitive freedom as against civilized repression, the symbol, in fact, of the entire primitive way of life as against the civilized way of life. What is the truth about the Dance as pure emotion and individual self-expression? On the formal side it may be said at once that the dance of primitive man has very little spontaneity and very little self-expression. The gestures and the movements and the accompaniment are hieratically fixed. The savage warrior who lets himself go in the tribal dance lets himself go in precisely the same bodily movements that his ancestors have practised for generations under the instruction and terror of the Medicine Man. Let us take the trouble to remember a truth stressed in all accounts of the primitive life, namely that the primitive man's dance is so largely ritual. We shall then understand how the introduction of a new spontaneous dance step or a new barytone motive by some individual dancer in Walarumbia would be very much like the injection of a few phrases of his own into the Twenty-sixth Psalm by a spontaneous member of Dr. Fosdick's congregation. The primitive code, the primitive etiquette, is a rigid thing.

Dancing for Business

But beyond the manner of the primitive dance is its matter, its meaning. That meaning, though often enough discussed, in vital moments escapes us. The dance of the jungle folk is not a dance at all, as we understand dancing. It is ritual, as we have seen; but it is more than ritual. It is strictly Business.

Primitive man lives surrounded by unseen powers who exercise control over his destinies and whom he seeks in turn to coerce or placate by magic and prayer. The dance is magic and prayer, directed to strictly utilitarian purposes. Primitive man dances in order to ensure the fertility of his fields and his womenfolk. He dances in order to bring rain. He dances in order to ward off the demons of plague. He dances to ensure a successful hunting expedition. He dances to ensure a successful head-hunting expedition. He dances, in short, for business reasons.

For us the parallel would be if the members of the New York Stock Exchange were to put on full dress at twelve noon and go through a programme of waltzes and two-steps in Battery Park in order to ensure an average rise of fifty points for one hundred selected Rails, Utilities, and Industrials in the next three months. Or suppose the Garment Trade were to dance up Eighth Avenue in order to ensure a healthy popular demand for the new crêpe de Chine afternoon gowns trimmed with kasha petit-point down the back and around the elbows. Or suppose Messrs. Chrysler, Sloan, Packard, and Studebaker were to dance all the way up Pennsylvania Avenue from the Capitol to the White House in order to invoke a divine blessing on their new 32-cylinder air-cooled shock absorber. When the traveler reports the natives of New Guinea dancing as usual, it means Business as Usual.

Correctly observed, a dance in the heart of the New Guinea jungle turns out to be that most dreadful of things, a meeting of the local Rotary Club. The Walarumbas rotate, not because they are care-free, but for the very practical reasons I have enumerated. But when the plain American business man, in surrender to a real play instinct, takes a week off from his business and arrays himself in the chaste red, green, yellow, and gold uniform of a Supersublime Magnificent Hyperpotentate of the Noble Order of Magoozlum, the critical temper in America suffers untold agonies at the sight. When the members of the Rotary luncheon club put their arms about each other's shoulders and spontaneously — yea, inexcusably — bawl "Sweet Adeline," the observer of the

American scene shudders. Sure, we want Release, Spontaneity, the Primitive Gesture; but always it must be *my* kind, not the American people's kind.

VII

HE IS STANDARDIZED

THERE is an American city of more than seven million inhabitants to which one visiting Englishman several years ago addressed a most touching farewell. "Good-bye," he said, "most beautiful of modern cities! Good-bye to glimmering spires and lighted bastions, dreamlike as the castles and cathedrals of a romantic vision!" Since the day when Henry W. Nevinson tore himself loose from glamorous New York, the city's sky line has been carried up to a point 1248 feet above the sidewalk at the corner of Fifth Avenue and Thirty-fourth Street. The number of lesser pinnacles, towers, turrets, bastions, battlements, and escarpments has so multiplied that a later Englishman spoke of New York City as in the total effect Babylonian. That is what Mr. Chesterton called it in the Christmas season of 1930.

But there is one thing which the visitor in his rapid survey of the largest American city cannot, perhaps, be expected to note, and which the people of New York are themselves too busy to note. It is this: although Alfred E. Smith's Empire State Building on Fifth Avenue is eighty-six stories high, the average height of all buildings in New York City is five and one-half stories. Half-a-dozen rivals press close on the heels — or is it the wings? — of the Empire State. The brick mountains of second rank are too numerous to mention, yet enough to elicit the wonder of the Europeans. The city's millions do spend their business hours moving through brick canyons, and their glimpse of the sky is indeed Babylon, when it is not Camelot or Chartres. Yet the average height of the New York building line is less than that of Paris.

The reason will of course have been grasped by the discerning reader. If New York teems with skyscrapers it must actually swarm with low structures. It does. For every one of its shining minarets the city must count a score of buildings that by comparison are hovels. It does. At the foot of Mt. Woolworth in the down-town district cluster the four-story brick domiciles of the aristocracy of the year 1825; these homes are now warehouses and factory "lofts." From the foot of Mt. Al Smith, at Fifth Avenue and Thirty-fourth Street, there run eastward along the latter thoroughfare two lines of the stately brownstone homes of the aristocracy of the year 1875, but after less than half a mile the exclusive brownstone melts into Third Avenue of the proletarians. The entire ten miles of Third Avenue, from its origins in the Bowery to its conclusion in the farthest Bronx, are lined with the dingy three- and four-story brick tenements of approximately the Civil War, subsiding, as Third Avenue draws nearer the Arctic Circle, to the two-and-a-half-story frame civilization of approximately 1880.

The roof line of New York as you see it from the selected point of view, from the harbor, the river, the bridges, the parks, is the spired and pinnacled host to which all hearts surrender, even those of her hard-boiled inhabitants. But the roof line of New York as you walk along the streets is like a mon- strously defaced ripsaw. A tooth 900 feet high stands close to a tooth 30 feet high upon which follows a tooth 550 feet high which hustles a "taxpayer" 20 feet high. And that is Manhattan Island, housing only one fourth of the city's permanent population. In the great bedroom borough of Brooklyn the people live at an average altitude, I imagine, of three stories. People by the scores of thousands emerge from thirty-six-story garment factories in Manhattan and go home to a two-story frame or double-family brick in Brooklyn.

That is New York. It has a nightmare roof line of mountain peaks and molehills. It does business a thousand feet up in the air, inside of monoliths of glass and steel and the stark flat surfaces that satisfy the modernist architect's yearning for that boyish figure. But it houses one third of its people in the old-law "dumb-bell" tenements, in a minimum of light and air. It is a city which rears new select residential skyscrapers in derelict neighborhoods, so that the apartment palaces stand rooted in tenements and lumber yards and gas tanks. It is a city where skyscrapers are also churches; where Egyptian obelisks are steam-radiator showrooms; where Roman basilicas are national banks; where Babylonian terraces are, as fate may have it, garment factories or apartments de luxe or Medical Centres or multiple-unit garages. It is a city in which 1930, discounting 1950, is cheek by jowl with 1860, with 1840.

And this vast outbreak of lawlessness and idiosyncrasy in brick and stone is the metropolis of a nation whose great sin, among several great sins, it is to be Standardized.

The Sectional Monotony of It All!

But wait a minute (the critical mind will say), you miss the point. When people complain of American life standardized and stereotyped, it is true that most of the complaining may come from New York, but the application and justification lie elsewhere. New York itself is sufficiently varied and amusing, at least for an American city. It is in interior America that monotony, flatness, regimentation, mass production, and mass consumption operate. When we speak of a people standardized into the same clothes, the same toothpastes, the same country clubs, the same gin parties, the same newspaper headlines, the same college stadiums, the same chambers of commerce, the same Knights of Magoozlum, the same garages and filling stations, the same go-getters, the same — well, when we speak of this dead level of uniformity, it is of the country beyond the Alleghanies that we speak. Our quarrel is with the Mississippi Valley which is so fond of being the heart of America, though a heart nearly one-half the size of the body should be an anatomical wonder.

Very well, then, let us take the heart of America. Let us go one thousand miles west from New York City into the very middle of the Middle West. Let us visit the state of Tennessee and the town of Dayton, and recall the summer of 1925 when certain court proceedings were under way in a Dayton courthouse upon which was focussed the attention of the world. Dayton, which prosecuted a young teacher named Scopes because he taught in his high-school science classes that man emerged out of lower animal forms in accordance with the laws of Evolution, and contrary to the laws of the State of Tennessee duly enacted — Dayton has a contribution to make to the subject of Standardized America.

Now the diversity of life exhibited by the English scene has always delighted the American traveler. He revels in the differences of tongue and manner — the broad-syllabled folk of Cornwall and Devon, the burr of Yorkshire, the Cockney singsong . . .

The diversity of the French scene is not unfamiliar to American tourists and readers: the hard-headed, shrewd Norman, the mystic Breton, the febrile folk of Provence, the dashing, flashing Gascon!

In lesser-known countries American admiration is evoked by the local color of dialect, costume, custom, tradition. How charmingly diversified are the several provinces of Czechoslovakia in the matter of embroidered aprons and blouses, village dances, homemade medical remedies, and other superstitions!

But when we find in the United States a local or regional peculiarity that is more than a variant, that is nothing short of a revolution, we are outraged.

How many of us have had the courage to render

to anti-Evolution Tennessee the applause that her extraordinary courage has so plainly earned? Tennessee went beyond local peculiarities in dress and dialect and cookery and dances on the village green to assert for herself nothing less than a Law of Nature all her own. Where, outside of Tennessee and Arkansas, with Mississippi and Florida aching to come in, has there been such a mighty challenge to the standardization imposed upon mankind by Charles Darwin? Where, outside of the United States, is there a state or a province or a shire or a *Bezirk* or a vilayet with sufficient individuality to insist on its own cosmic order? We have yet to hear that Liverpool refuses to subscribe to the same earth's orbit of 365¼ days around the sun that Edinburgh acknowledges. Marseilles has not rejected the gravitational system that is in vogue at Lyons and Bordeaux. Berlin has not split with Munich on the question of the exact boiling point of water at sea level, or the proper place of hydrogen in the Atomic Table.

But in this country we do insist that the laws of biology are subject to the police power of the State. This may be perversity, as it is obviously benightedness; but surely it is not subservience, it is not regimentation. "I appeal from your customs," says Tennessee. "I hereby enact that beginning at noon

January 1 the square on the hypothenuse of a right-angle triangle shall not be equal to the sum of the squares on the other two sides, but equal to 2.3 times the sum of said squares, subject to a penalty of $500 fine, or six months in the calaboose, or both." Life in Tennessee, far from being standardized, is thus shown to be as fresh, as unspoiled, as among the most primitive of the Protochukchis. Imagine a New York hostess introducing an old friend from Tennessee. She says, "Maud, dear, I want you to meet Mr. Hoskison from Nashville, though how he can live in that standardized environment is more than I can imagine. Why, in Nashville, Maud, they think the sun moves around the earth." And to another friend our hostess might say, "Estelle, dear, I want you to meet Mr. Hoskison from Knoxville, where people don't dare for a moment to be themselves. They believe the world was created in six days in 4004 B. C."

The Crushing Burden of Non-Enforcement

But wait a moment (the critical temper will say); that is all very clever about Tennessee, but you quite miss the point of the Dayton trial. What matters is not so much the particular doctrine that Tennessee has established by act of Legislature as the fact that she should attempt to establish any scientific doctrine by legislative fiat. Is not this the heart and kernel of American standardization? The Monkey Trial was only the fine flower of our American fondness for passing laws to make people uniformly good, or uniformly orthodox, or uniformly sober, or uniformly patriotic. If Tennessee had the power, as she doubtless has the will, she would pass a law making every person in the United States believe in a flat earth standing still and the sun going around it, and Adam falling asleep and losing a rib. If Tennessee in 1925 prohibited the origin of species and the descent of man, it was largely because Tennessee drew courage and inspiration from that other celebrated law to prohibit. . . .

The answer is, yes, my friend, we do pass all kinds of regulatory laws. But what do we do with the laws after we pass them? Laws to prohibit and laws to compel, laws to punish and laws to absolve and abate, we enact them and we disregard them. Of all civilized peoples we are far and away the most lawless; and of this fact we are aware, consciously or unconsciously, when we enact the laws which we proceed to disobey. Precisely because we know in advance that the law we establish will be observed by those who choose to do so, and will be violated by those who will, we go at the business of lawmaking with a light heart. Implicit in the Tennessee

Monkey Law was the assurance that those Tennessee citizens who could not get along without their Darwin would manage to satisfy their needs without undue hardship. At the same time the anti-Darwin citizenship would have the joy and profit of an anti-Darwin law. The Tennessee law, like so many of our laws, did not really attempt to impose a standard, but only to assert an opinion or a hope. Tennessee declared her independence of the International Scientists, just as Iowa and Idaho love to declare their independence of the International Bankers, for the purpose of going on record, rather than in any real expectation of results.

In any case, Tennessee seceded from a world-wide formula; and it is Tennessee's critics who are the real foes of liberty, the real standardizers.

We are the most lawless people on earth; which is to say we are of all peoples the least standardized, since order, uniformity, monotony, are the essence of Law. The unvarying sameness with which Englishmen, Frenchmen, and Germans obey the laws of their country is a blight which we have, more or less happily, escaped. At the risk of becoming tiresome about Prohibition, we may recall that the Eighteenth Amendment as a force for standardization is not in the least what the indictments usually charge: provided, that is, we distinguish between what Prohibition tries to be and what it succeeds in being.

It may be readily conceded that Volstead connotes the most ambitious attempt in history to regiment and standardize a whole people, certainly since Peter the Great prescribed the statutory length of whiskers in Russia. But in practice the effect of Volstead has been to reveal America as the very antithesis of a flat ethnic monotone. Has Prohibition reduced a particular set of American habits to a rigid pattern, or has Prohibition only illuminated and accentuated deep-seated diversities in the national life? On the Prohibition issue we have seen the American people divided: (1) city against village and farm; (2) North and East against South and West; (3) Protestant against Catholic; (4) pro-Volstead Big Industry against anti-Volstead Small Industry and Trade; (5) native-born against foreign-born, and so forth. By the Prohibition test we are not a drill squad, but a chaos.

Lock Step or License?

Another test of standardization, even sharper, perhaps, than the ordeal by Volstead, is to be found in the various discoveries of America's "soul" as a result of the World War. One of such post-bellum revelations was this very Standardization with which we are now concerned. The war ushered in a decade of self-analysis, social satire, drastic revaluation of existing American values; and foremost among the causes of the great discontent that seized upon the young and the forward-looking after the Armistice was the withering dullness of American life arising in such large measure from its sameness. The life of the intellect and the emotions in these United States was carefully examined and found to be feeble, gray, and thin, because the people were so thoroughly standardized.

But this was not the sole discovery. At the very time that a young rebel generation had the scales shaken from its eyes by the impact of war, and found itself living in an America gone stale with uniformity, a quite opposite set of scales was falling from a different set of eyes. A great many Americans were dumbfounded to learn from the war that America was not a nation but a heterogeneous mob. The young rebel generation bemoaned the fact that the country had either been drill-sergeanted into the war or had plunged into the war under the whip of herd instinct. Their elders were simultaneously horrified to think that America's reluctant entrance into the war showed that we were not a united people thinking nationally. We were an aggregation of sectionalisms, localisms, racialisms, conflicting traditions and sentimental allegiances. In one camp you heard outcries against this thing called Americanization, which laid its heavy hand on the children of a dozen colorful immigrant races and, by means of the public school, the safety razor, and the Keencut Klassy Klothes, flattened them into the dull pattern of the native-born. In the other camp there was panic because Americanization had broken down, because the Melting Pot had melted nothing.

As between these of us who saw in American diversity a national peril, and those in whose mouth the phrase "100 per cent American" became a conventional jeer, who was right? Are we, by this test of the war, overstandardized, to the bitter sorrow of the Liberal weeklies, or undigested and unassimilated, as the D.A.R. think they have only too good reason to fear? Well, fortunately for the comfort and peace of mind of the present writer, an answer is not necessary for the purpose of the present argument. The mere fact that you have Americans violently disagreeing about Standardization is enough to show that we are not standardized. What more can you demand in the way of variety than one section of the American people pointing with pride to what another section views with alarm? Surely the cloak of a deadening uniformity has not enveloped and confined the limbs of a nation which differs so rudely on which is the greater peril — the Alien or the Ancestor.

Life and the Spring Fashions

The misunderstanding of Jones, in the sample or in the mass, is the result, as I have had occasion to insist so often, of looking too deep down into Jones or not deep enough. It is either deep down into Jones's glands and complexes or else it's a hurried glance at the front page of Jones's newspaper without going to the trouble of looking through the whole paper. In this present matter of the Standardization of Jones we have not looked deep enough. Everywhere in the United States it is observed that Jones lives in the same hotel room with private bath, travels in the same Pullman lower, wears the same Fashion Bilt clothes, pores over the same comic strip, plays the same golf, drinks the same illegal mixtures, orates on the same City Beautiful project, dilates before the same business-club luncheons. But we have made the slight mistake of assuming that the same heart beats under the Universal Two-Button Sack Suit That Is Different in Tallapoosa, Alabama, and in Madison, Wisconsin. Yet how often it is a different heart, mind, and set of loyalties! There is still a type and tradition that may be called New England, the South, the Northwest Territory, the

Far West. The standardized newspaper presents the same standardized headlines in Dallas, Texas, and in Rochester, New York. But we have seen in recent years what a lively variety exists as between Texas and New York.

If it were not the rule that in appraising America there shall be no corrective check by other countries, one might put this question: Where is there another country that prints and consumes so many diversified maps, charts, and graphs illustrating the Distribution of Things by sections and by States? They are charts running from the deepest black to the purest white, with all intermediate stages in shades, dots, horizontal lines, vertical lines, crosshatchings from right to left, crosshatchings from left to right — all of them testifying to a range of variation under one flag that is often more than variation, that is often chaos. The Lynching Map of the United States shows Georgia black and Vermont snow white. The Automobile Map shows New York and Pennsylvania and California black, but Mississippi only faintly gray. On the history of the last ten years consult your Income Tax Map, College Map, Literacy Map, Indian Reservation Map, Atlantic Monthly Map, Native-Born of Foreign Parentage Map, Rural Doctors Map, Fundamentalist-Modernist Map, Homicide Map — for even in the art of murder, which, next to the art of the skyscraper, we have developed beyond all rivalry, there is extraordinary variation in the United States. . . .

· Yes, even in our killings we are not standardized; but range all the way from a miserly three murders per one hundred thousand inhabitants in Boston to seventy murders per one hundred thousand in Memphis. It shows that even in respect to traits peculiarly American the writers have emphasized the sameness and have overlooked the differences. We note that the Sunday comics are studied in New York and in Kansas. We note that in Oregon and in Florida occur the same nationally known biscuits, tooth pastes, tiled bathrooms, and skyscrapers. But we have declined to notice that the popularity of Sunday comics after all varies greatly between New York and Kansas. The per capita consumption of tiled bathrooms shows a striking rate of variation between California and South Carolina. The skyscraper rate per thousand of the population is far different in New York and in Idaho. And only forty miles from New York City, inside of the commuting zone and in villages economically dominated by the commuter, you find the authentic New England, that New England which is still so largely itself. And the South still waits to be ironed out in respect to its "soul," though not in respect to its cotton mills and skyscrapers. And the Indianapolis of 1931 is still strongly reminiscent of 1880. . . .

The Monotony of Europe

Well, always it comes down to this lack of a comparative criticism, this failure to appraise American monotony like other things in America by the facts of monotony elsewhere. Even Mr. Nevinson, who is in love with New York's fairy towers, takes a slam at our sameness. He is going back, he says, to a land of old villages and towns, "as little like each other as one woman is like the next." To his trained native eye the variety between European village and European village may be there. But what difference is there for the American visitor between one small French town and another — the same red brick or bleached stucco, the same Place d'Armes with the plane trees and the band stand, the same cafés, the same little round tables. The reader may himself make the experiment, on a larger scale. Let him turn to the pictures in his Sunday paper for the latest Fascist riot or Communist upflare or anti-Semitic demonstration, and let him guess from the looks of the scene what city it is. Berlin or Bucharest, Rome, Madrid, Danzig, Paris, Leipzig, Sofia, Athens — he will see the same principal street or square flanked by the same six-story apartment houses with mansard roof and French windows and ornamental balconies; and in the streets the same cafés with little round tables and bent cane chairs; and, dominating the whole scene, the same big legends recommending Underwood or Kodak or Bovril or Apéritif or Tabac. How the more ardent inhabitants of the Avenue Victor-Hugo and the Friedrichstrasse must long to get away from all this eternal sameness!

The monotony of Europe is a dreadful thing. We have it on good authority that France to-day, in the matter of public education, is still what it was years ago when a Minister of Public Instruction had only to look at the clock, and if it was 10.35 then he knew that in fifty thousand elementary schools several million children were all studying the reign of Louis XIV. But if in the United States you looked at the clock and saw it was 10.35, then in Boston the children might be studying the battle of Concord, and in New York it would be algebraic equations with one unknown quantity, and in Pennsylvania something about Human Relations, and in Arizona spelling, and in California perhaps boat building, and in Chicago the Gettysburg Address, and in Oregon self-expression; and for several million Appalachian Mountain whites and Deep South Negroes there would be no schools at all, or almost none. America is the land where hundred-million-dollar college endowments and five million illiterates blend into one unbroken monotone for the trained observer — the sufficiently trained observer.

Such is the Standardization of America as between place and place. This is the horizontal standardization of three million square miles of territory against which the outcry has been raised. But what the outcriers really have in mind — and possibly deplore — is vertical standardization in the United States. The sameness complained of is that prevailing between high and low, between the shop girl and the millionaire's wife, both in furs, between the shop girl's father and the millionaire husband, both using the same ideas and language. This standardization is a different matter altogether. It is the Standardization of Democracy and may bear further looking into.

VIII

JONES AND THE CONTROL
EXPERIMENT

"HE spent the remainder of his life in the toil of building up a vast satire on the futility of human knowledge and the omnipresence of mediocrity. This is the depressing and bewildering *Bouvard et Pécuchet.*"

My quotation is from a great literary critic, the late Edmund Gosse, writing in a late edition of the *Encyclopædia Britannica.* The man of whom Gosse is speaking is the late Gustave Flaubert, a Frenchman. He wrote *Madame Bovary, Salammbô,* and the enchanting *Temptation of Saint Anthony,* and died in the year 1880. The scene to which Flaubert turned for the raw materials of a study in human stupidity was naturally the country he knew best — his own, France. His two heroes, Bouvard and Pécuchet, are *petits bourgeois* of Paris who pass their leisure in each other's company on the quay benches, discoursing on the news of the day and on the basic truths of life underlying the newspaper. Flaubert died before the book was finished. But he lived long enough to create a devastating picture of the purblind vision, the flat emotion, the ignorance, the drab, drear waste and monotony that are the "bourgeois soul."

In other words, probably the most savage and destructive evocation ever achieved of the soul of Main Street is the work of a French observer writing of a street called Boulevard Bourdon in a town called Paris.

We may now turn for a few minutes to another point of the compass. Having met the requirements of scholarly research by delving into a source so little accessible to the general public as the *Encyclopædia Britannica,* consistency demands that my next quotation be from an authority at least equally unapproachable, namely, Webster's New International Dictionary. Here the desired quotation is as follows: —

Control Experiment: An experiment whose object is to enable the experimenter to control or check the results of other experiments. By imitating the conditions of the other experiments with the exception of some particular, inferences can be obtained as to how far the omitted factor was responsible for the results observed in the other cases.

This is a precise statement, if a trifle heavy perhaps. Suppose . . .

. . . It is hardly necessary to state that everything that follows is my own, and not from Webster's New International; though I trust the spelling of the words will be found not to depart too widely from that well-thought-of publication. . . .

Suppose, then, you have a theory that by exposing white mice to the violet ray you can teach them to sing. Suppose you subject several dozen white mice to the violet treatment, and they do begin to sing. Have you made out your case? Have you added to the sum of human knowledge?

Not yet, if you have been trained in the methods of rigorous scientific experimentation and research. The outburst of your mice into song may, after all, be due to some other agency than the violet ray; an unknown agency, an unsuspected agency, a supremely accidental agency, but still it is there. The phenomenon of the singing mice may have been produced by a peculiar condition of the atmosphere that will occur once in ten thousand years, that will last a split second, but that will nevertheless turn the trick. Or it may have been something that got into the food; you will remember what happened to poor Dr. Jekyll-Hyde as the result of an accidental impurity in his medicine. Or it may have been a mysterious and unobserved change in the blood of the little animals, due to the appearance of a new activity in the nearer star nebulæ; who will say no, in this incomprehensible new universe of ours?

Well, to eliminate all accident, the well-trained laboratory worker always conducts his experiments with two batches of mice. The two groups are fed on exactly the same food, kept in exactly the same room temperature, subjected to the same treatment in every painful particular, except one. The violet-ray treatment is administered to one group of mice and is withheld from the other group, the "control" group. If, under these circumstances and precautions, the violet-ray mice begin to sing, and the others do not, you are scientifically justified in concluding that it is the rays that made the difference; seeing that they are the only difference of which you are aware.

So, when you are studying the effects of nitrogen fertilizer on the growth of corn, you plant in adjacent flowerpots or beds some fertilized corn and some unfertilized corn and tend them with the same exact care in every other particular. You are then justified in saying that the taller corn is due to the nitrogen stimulus.

So, when you think you have discovered a serum against diphtheria you will not be content with the results from guinea pigs and rabbits and mice. You must be hard-hearted enough, on the final test, to withhold what you believe to be the life-giving serum from a sufficient number of children sick with diphtheria, while administering the serum to other diphtheric children. If the treated children get well and the untreated control children do not, you are justified in believing that you have made a discovery. You are not so justified until you have condemned your control children to the peril of death. Readers of *Arrowsmith* will recall such a poignant situation.

In every branch of scientific research the control experiment has become established routine. Before you announce that the violet ray causes mice to sing you will look about you carefully. You will of course give considerable thought to the mice who have had the ray and have refused to sing. You will give still more thought — and that is the control experiment — to mice who have not had the ray and yet develop musical powers.

In the Same Boat

It is only in the matter of affirming big new "truths" about human beings in the mass that we are still painfully backward in the use of the control method. Well, of course, sociologists and economists and publicists are in no position as yet to take several million people and experiment with them, using a million of them as a control on the rest. But the sociologists and the economists and the rest do sin against the scientific method by refusing to avail themselves of the control facilities which nature has already provided, though in a form, to be sure, a good deal short of the scientific ideal.

For instance: Before you announce to the world your discovery of Main Streetitis as a peculiarly American disease it should not be difficult to look about for any other nation, people, or race that may be similarly afflicted. If in the course of such an inquiry you encounter Flaubert's *Bouvard et Pécuchet,* or, for that matter, his much-better-known *Madame Bovary,* which deals with small-town life in France, the least you can do, as a conscientious inquirer into American mass life, is to look thoughtful.

To be sure, the situation to-day is not a hopeless one. We are beginning to recognize the value of the control experiment, and now and then some interesting results are recorded. (And may I be permitted to say that from now on I shall take the liberty to use "control" in a somewhat less rigorous, though I think sufficiently proper, sense, as describing the general idea of Comparison?)

When the unscientific mind asserts that we have

Prohibition and we have Prosperity and that therefore Prohibition has produced Prosperity, we may
apply the control-comparison method in a number
of ways: (1) We look a little deeper into American facts of the last ten years to see whether prosperity may not be due in some degree to high wages
since 1920; or to the war; or to more women in
gainful occupations with a consequent increase in
family income; or to the rise of new industries like
the automobile and the moving pictures. (2) We
look abroad to see whether there are any countries
which have not adopted prohibition, but have
nevertheless advanced in prosperity since the war.
(3) We take another look at our own country
to see whether one may have prohibition without
having prosperity. The first two tests were applied
by the Wickersham Commission with impressive
results.

We are beginning to make use of the comparative
method; but of course it is a very thin beginning.
It needed an elaborate and expensive Wickersham
Commission to do a bit of comparison work on
prohibition. It is still a very rare thing, for instance,
to find the comparative method applied to that other
contemporary experiment in high-pressure salvation
— namely, Soviet Russia.

When the achievements of Russia under Communist rule are exhibited for the admiring wonder of the world, the principle of control would suggest that we compare twelve years of Russian progress under Communism with the average progress registered in the non-Communized countries of the world since the Armistice.

When awe-struck observers come back from Russia to report that in the land of the Soviets they have that extraordinary innovation known as maternity benefits, it might be useful to know that maternity insurance exists in Great Britain, France, Germany, Italy, Mexico, and so on, and not excluding Tokyo and Shanghai.

Yes, we have made a beginning with the comparative method. But for a generation which has been so eager to substitute the "scientific control" of human destiny for the haphazard way in which people have lived up to now, we have been remarkably indifferent to that much humbler form of control which we have been discussing, the control of Formula by Fact.

Imbecility among the Nations

From the backwoods newspapers of the American people you garner in the course of a month perhaps a dozen pages of stupidity, illiteracy of speech and thought, parochialism, obscurantism, the ugly, the grotesque, the mean, the comic; you bring together a month's harvest of bad metaphors, lame puns, bulls, *lapsus linguæ,* Spoonerisms, and all the other verbal misbehaviors of 122,000,000 people; and you label the result "Americana." But we have seen what Gustave Flaubert did with the imbecilities of Frenchmen. And perhaps we may recall what Jonathan Swift did with the stupidity and meanness of Englishmen and Irishmen. And so we might get back to the times when Aristophanes found plenty of material for his collection of humanity's intellectual and moral limitations among the most learned and cultured people that ever lived.

The doctrine of comparison forbids the labeling as Americana of universal human follies that are also Gallicana, Anglicana, and Atheniana. And that is all which the principle does demand. It has no quarrel with the contents of the satirical package, but only with the label. It recognizes that the lashing of American fools is the business of American satirists. They will find the job big enough, and may properly leave the French people to their own Flauberts and the British to their own Swifts. The American satirist is welcome to go ahead and lay about him; but he is not at liberty to misbrand. He is free to denounce greed, cowardice, ignorance, cruelty, oppression, mediocrity, as these ugly heads rear themselves in America. He may not call them Americana and thereby suggest that they are this nation's peculiar plagues.

"He despised," says Edmond Gosse of Gustave Flaubert, "his fellow men, their habits, their lack of intelligence, their contempt for beauty, with a passionate scorn which has been compared to that of an ascetic monk." Now if there is one sin that towers above all others in the Americana indictments, it is the American people's incapacity for recognizing and feeling Beauty as other nations feel it; notably, in these recent years, as the French people feel beauty. The difference is that Flaubert saw in his countrymen the ridiculous and contemptible thing called Man. But among us the faults are not human but American.

Well, now, on second thought, perhaps it is unjust to insist that the satirist shall be careful with his labels. In the heat of his trade it may be too much to ask that he observe the proprieties and the shades of meaning. It may be his privilege to lay it on thick and not to waste time making fine distinctions between sinning Americans and Americans' sins. After all, it would be too much to have Isaiah pause to remark that the daughters of Zion were not the only ones to walk with outstretched necks and wanton eyes and making a tinkling with their feet.

The daughters of Nineveh and Tyre and Sidon might be just as up to date, but Isaiah's business was primarily with Jerusalem, and he may be forgiven for characterizing bold looks and affected gaits and tinkling anklets as Jerusalemiana.

But again we are driven back to our principal source of concern and favorite *bêtes noires,* the serious students of Society. They will grow angry if you call them satirists. They are dispassionate observers working in the spirit of science. Of them we surely have the right to demand that in making statements about the American people and American civilization they shall observe the principle of control.

For Instance —

1. Materialism: A truly scientific study of American materialism and success worship is not complete unless it takes brief notice of the celebrated French qualities of prudence and thrift as studied by Balzac and Zola in the French peasant, and by countless French writers in their *petite bourgeoisie.* Specifically, it would be instructive to take the way in which the materialistic American marries and compare it with the circumstances attending the typical Continental marriage — and not in France only — in the matter of dowry, family connections, and

other prudentialities. It is, I believe, still the French law that no male under the age of twenty-five may pick himself a wife without the consent of the "family council."

2. Main Street: A just evaluation of Main Street would demand a glance, at least, at other Main Streets. The Main Street of Gustave Flaubert is the point we started from. The Main Street of George Gissing and of Arnold Bennett might have something to teach us. Or one might dip into the Russian Main Streets of Anton Chekhov, in whom our own refugees from Main Street have found so much comfort. In Chekhov's pages the theme of the Provincial is ever present. The stagnancy, the futility, the absurdity, and the pathos of provincial life are a familiar theme in every European literature. It extends beyond Europe and modern times to every civilization that developed cities. The Athenians had their yokels in the Bœotians. The Egyptian papyri compare the delightful life of the scribe — the city feller — with that of the peasant and the soldier. The American provincial is part of a universal tradition.

3. Publicity: In respect to the Advertising evil in American life and this whole business of high-pressure salesmanship, perhaps it would be fair to snatch a moment for a glance at British commercial

civilization as pictured by H. G. Wells, in *Tono Bungay*.

4. Business Ethics: In measuring the processes of tooth and claw among America's business Titans one might pause a moment to recall the late Octave Mirbeau's play *Les affaires sont les affaires,* familiar to an elder generation of Americans as *Business Is Business.* And a help to the proper ·perspective on American civilization of the Jay Gould and Jim Fiske period may be found in the history of the Panama Affair in France and the long succession of British get-rich-quick episodes — Whitaker Wright, Hatry, and so forth.

5. Censorship: Before getting utterly downhearted about the censorship blight in America one might stop to ponder, for a little while, censorship in Ireland, censorship in Germany, censorship in France, — where Flaubert and Baudelaire fell foul of the censor, — and censorship in ancient Athens, where it scored a very notable hit in the person of one Socrates. He was put to death on the charge of corrupting the youth of Athens. To accuse anyone of corrupting the youth of New York or of Boston or Indianapolis is, of course, to speak in the tongue of barbarians and smut-hounds.

6. Deportation: The business of expelling from the country a few loud-mouthed alien Reds, lest they

overthrow the nation of 122,000,000 people builded by Washington, Jefferson, and Lincoln, is not a spectacle to make one's bosom swell with pride. But as to the ethics and æsthetics of deportation I find myself brought to a halt by the thought, again, of Athens, the violet-crowned, radiant with culture and pagan freedom. Have we forgotten the high-school textbook on Ostracism? If a certain number of Athenian voters demanded exile for any citizen, out he must go, without being accused of any offense, without any imputation against his character. For the good of the State he went out, deported, ostracized. And you may remember the free and unterrified Athenian voter who cast his ballot — his potsherd or *ostrakon* — in favor of deporting Aristides the Just. "I am tired of hearing him called the Just." Yet Athens made quite a name for herself in the arts and other forms of self-expression.

7. Brag: Before picking up the whip to flay this notorious American habit of boastfulness, this fondness for making the eagle scream, a conscientious inquirer will do two things: —

(*a*) He will try to get down to something like the statistical facts about American brag. Out of every one hundred Americans who visit Europe, how many really go about slapping Prime Ministers on the back and telling them how much better we do things in the Board of Aldermen back home in Seattle; how many Americans really go about Paris tearing up hundred-franc notes to show their contempt for the ridiculous currencies of the foreigners; how many raucous Americans hang over the American Bars in Europe's hotels telling the world about home? And, on the other hand, how many of these one hundred sample Americans go about Europe quite shy, devout, awed by a spectacle and a tradition to whose splendor they bear tribute precisely when they say that after all there is no place like home? By this they do not mean that the Second Presbyterian edifice back home is a finer thing than Chartres. They mean, quite humbly, that you Europeans have this wonderful Chartres which we have not, but after all it is so comfortable at home.

(*b*) When a statistical basis for American strut and swagger has been approximated; when we have found out, roughly, how many out of every traveling one hundred Americans go about Europe commenting with loud-mouthed candor, we might ask what the corresponding ratio might be among one hundred Englishmen or Frenchmen or Germans. American boastfulness would be compared with the much quieter but ever so much more effective British arrogance; or with the unshaken faith, in which every Parisian is born and dies, that outside of France a truly human existence is inconceivable.

8. Regimentation: Before pronouncing sentence on our over-organized, over-standardized, over-patternized American life, the just judge will give a thought to the rôle which precedent, order, and propriety play in the life of the normal German citizen who is *Verboten;* of the Englishman at his Public School where It Simply is n't Done; and of the Frenchman of twenty-five, who, as I said a little while ago, cannot marry without the consent of his Papa and his Maman.

Rigging the Game

In the reappraisal of American values after the war, the principle of the control experiment, the principle known to older scholars as the comparative method, was neglected. This does not mean that America was not brought into juxtaposition with other countries. That was always being done. But it was not the honest comparison which places two objects side by side and studies them objectively for resemblances as well as for differences. There flourished a fraudulent comparative method. The method pretended to be comparison, but the real aim was contrast. There was no desire to find out the likenesses between America and others. There was a veritable lust for establishing the divergencies, the fatal divergencies — for America.

A prize fighter whose manager matches him out of his class against a hopelessly superior opponent is said to be overmatched. The noble art of over-matching America flourished during the decade of the 1920's. Regularly she was matched to her disadvantage, rarely to her advantage. Was it a question of personal liberty? Then the contrast was drawn with France, where people would not think of having their dinner without their wine, or with Germany and England, where beer is a food. But very seldom, in discussing personal liberty, was America compared with personal liberty in Italy under Mussolini and in Russia under Stalin. On the other hand, if it was a question of demonstrating the anarchy of the capitalist system at its highest point of development in the United States, the comparison was not with France or Germany or England, which are also capitalistic. Anarchy in the American economic system was brought into contrast with the system of regulated, orderly production in Italy and in Soviet Russia.

Obviously, with all the world to pick from, there was never any trouble in finding a place where things are better done than in the United States.

In personal liberty we are below the French, but it was not thought necessary to mention that in kindliness and fraternity we are the superiors of the French. In discipline we are inferior to Fascist Italy, but it was not thought necessary to mention that we are ever so much freer than the Italians. In family cohesion Americans are inferior to the Chinese, but it was not thought necessary to mention that in patriotism, in social solidarity, Americans are superior to the Chinese. In a love for the Beautiful the American people are undeniably in the kindergarten class compared with the divine Greeks. But nowhere was it thought necessary to point out that in physical courage, in zest for adventure, in a passionate love for novelty, in gregariousness, in love of physical exercises and the out-of-doors, Americans are the equals of the ancient Greeks. It is by no means certain that if Alcibiades came to New York he would spend his whole day crying shame upon our pruderies and our repressions. Part of the time Alcibiades might be up at the Yankee Stadium watching Babe Ruth.

This game of overmatching America by getting her into the ring against a foreign opponent two feet taller and one hundred pounds heavier was a sufficiently popular game in the last decade. But even more common was the practice of matching the

United States, not against a specific opponent, but against simply "Europe." When in the course of your monthly stalk through the American newspapers in pursuit of Americana you came across a choice bit in the pages of the *Pueblo* (California) *Sentinel,* you went on to contrast the Pueblo (California) Mind with the "European" Mind. But what is even worse, the Europe that was always being invoked or assumed for our discomfiture was in most cases a very special kind of Europe. America under the particular blight, let us say, of Methodism was not compared with a Europe synthesized and averaged out of the religious life of England, Germany, France, Italy, Scandinavia, Holland, Switzerland, Central Europe, and the Balkans. It was compared with a Europe produced by an act of special creation out of carefully selected materials. America of the Puritans, of the repressions, of the oppressions, of Main Street, of the Machines, of Wall Street, was at bottom being matched against an imaginary land across the seas to which one might apply the odd and awkward but sufficiently descriptive name of Parisia-Dostoievska.

If you will think back over the era of the 1920's, or for that matter if you will carefully observe its survivals to-day, reaching like wet tongues of a retreating tide into the dry sands, you will note that revolt from America was, and is, toward a very special kind of Europe. Young Americans did not expatriate themselves to make their home in London. Fugitives from the Puritan curfew engineers did not seek for a new way of life in Berlin. From the drabness of Iowa and Southern California ardent souls did not recoil to Oslo or Geneva or Bucharest. The challenge and the test for American values were derived from this synthetic European fatherland created by a union of the way of life as pursued in the French capital and the experiences of the celebrated Slav Soul. Behavior in Main Street was set up against behavior on the Left Bank. The emotional life of a dues-paying member of the Anti-Saloon League was tested by the soul waves of Dmitri Karamazov.

Paris-Dostoievsky Land

Why Parisia-Dostoievska should become the yardstick for America, applied by a rebel American generation terribly in earnest, is not hard to understand. The actual Paris is by tradition the capital of European culture. It is by equally strong tradition the refuge of dissenters, rebels, and refugees from other lands. Paris is the home of European experimentation in the arts and, to a lesser extent, in politics. This is a rule to which, up to the World War, America was an exception. Our own earlier rebels and secessionists used to head, not for Paris, but for London — Whistler, Sargent, Henry James. But the war did bring a great many American young men to Paris; and they liked it.

Once established in Paris, either in the body or by spiritual filaments from Iowa, Chicago, and lower Manhattan, the refugees from the Puritan order would soon discover that in Paris you can let yourselves go in many different directions, but by no means in all directions. The French, as we have seen, have their own very rigid codes and proprieties and inhibitions. But the Russian Soul, as it manifested itself, not in the all-embracing vision of Tolstoy, not in the exquisite restraint of Turgeniev, not in the laughter of Gogol, but in the tortured if splendid visions of Dostoievsky, was a soul that let itself go all the way and in every direction. In the years before the war Dostoievsky gained a vogue in England, where he found imitators among the young men — Beresford, Walpole, Mackenzie, Canaan. After the war young Americans caught the impact of Dostoievsky; and caught it in the characteristic American way: hitting the line hard, getting all together now, fellows, for that last goal we must have. Are you ready? Let's go! Hitting on all sixteen cylinders; the way things are normally done in the U.S.A. Our insurgent youth went hell-bent for Dostoievsky's psychic hospital.

The Missing Guest

But even more striking, it seems to me, than the evocation of a synthetic Gallo-Slavic "Europe" for the testing of America was the practice of omitting from the argument the one foreign country which you would naturally expect to see set up as a real test for America. And that country is, of course, England.

At the serious risk of becoming a bore I shall venture to restate in a few words the central idea of the control experiment. It is this: the experiment which you use as a control, as a check on your original experiment, must differ in only one particular from the original experiment. You do not control violet-rayed mice in a Philadelphia laboratory by unrayed mice in a Tokyo laboratory. You do not check fertilized cotton in Texas by unfertilized cotton in the Sudan. Certainly you do not check fertilized wheat in Argentina by unfertilized cotton in the Sudan. The true method of comparison is between things not quite alike, but not too unlike. What comparison can there be, after all, between America and China? You are immediately beset by so many differences that you do not know where to begin. The essentials of their common humanity are present in the two peoples, but that much we knew beforehand. Beyond that the divergencies overwhelm the resemblances, and American values and Chinese values become incommensurable. This has been the vice of Paris-Dostoievsky Land as a test for America. The differences between that synthetic Europe and America are so many and so striking as to make any comparison between the two countries tremendously difficult — and not very useful. The overmatchers went too far for their own good. Who in the long run would pay to see a featherweight tackle a heavy-weight?

But of all countries England stands closest to America. And it is precisely England and the English that have counted least in the testing of American values by comparison with other nations. It would be absurd to say, of course, that England has not figured in the story of the last ten years. She has been cited as a witness for personal liberty against American regimentation. The British Labor Party has been popular with those engaged in showing up our own ridiculous party system. English amateur athletics have been mobilized against American professionalism. But in the general effect the civilization of England, the English mores and folkways, have not loomed big in the great assize of American civilization in these last ten years. In the appraisal of America, one would say offhand, Budapest has been more prominent than London.

Why? For the very reason, I suspect, that English civilization is in so many ways like American civilization. Particularly is it true that the English temper and mores are very like our own in respect to the particular interest that has loomed biggest in the testing of America. That is, of course, the question of sex. Vast quantities of words have been uttered about American prohibition, and patrioteering, and censorship, and commercialism, and mechanization and regimentation and materialism. But it is commonplace that the rebellion of the 1920's was chiefly concerned with the assertion of a new code of sex behavior, and certainly a new, freer vocabulary for the discussion of sex. The war against Puritanism was predominantly a war against the Puritan's ideas on sex.

It is now obvious why England as a yardstick for America would not do at all. The English, to be sure, have in their aristocratic caste plenty of material for anti-Puritan experimentation, as we may see in the world of Aldous Huxley. But if London has always had its smart set, free to live as it pleases, the tone of British life is still determined by its "respectable" middle classes. Noticeable modifications in English morals and manners have been produced by the war, but England is still in her mass life following the Puritan way of life. James Joyce, a refugee from a free but pious Ireland, goes to Paris, not to London, and his *Ulysses* is banned by the British censor. England could not be featured in the testing of America because the results might be "unfavorable." If you compared behavior in Indianapolis with behavior near Clapham Common, or if you tested the emotional life of Zenith by the emotional atmosphere of Arnold Bennett's Five Towns, there might be a different story to tell about American civilization as a freak or a tragedy.

England had to be absent from the American-European story, because England could not meet the requirements of a perfect shillalah to swing over the American pate. How could one play up the incubus of the Puritan spirit on creative art in America when England has a playwright named Bernard Shaw who is an arch-Puritan; or in the face of an English censor who only the other day sanctioned *Mrs. Warren's Profession,* and who will not yet permit the Creator to be shown on the stage; or in the face of a British Labor Party which, on its spiritual side, is virtually an Evangelistic organization?

In scoring American commercialism you could not very well mention the England of Business as

Usual. In scoring American sterility in the arts of painting and music you could not mention England, which in such matters has pulled a very light oar these hundred years. In scoring American play habits you might mention England; but only for the purpose of contrasting England's gentlemen amateurs with America's vicarious audiences at professional baseball games. But you must not mention England's vicarious audiences of 150,000 people at a professional football match.

Perhaps Then —

The intelligent reader will not have misunderstood me. It is not in the least the contention here that because England is in so many ways like America, it lets America out. It may only prove that England is not what she should be. It does not help us that we are found to be inhibited like the English, hypocrites and mealy-mouths like the English, enemies to art and the richer life, slaves of material worship, like the English. It may only mean that England stands badly in need of a decade of muckraking and soul searching.

Yet the thought that insists on obtruding is this: England, despite the very serious handicaps which she is now discovered to be sharing with America, has managed to cut quite a figure in the life of the mind and of the spirit these last two hundred years. At the same time with Methodism the English produced Wordsworth and Blake. At the same time with the Factory System they produced Shelley. To show that they have not yet lost this capacity for combining Puritanism with genius there are to-day Kipling and Shaw among the living and Thomas Hardy among the recent dead. Perhaps, then, to be mealy-mouthed about sex is after all only a racial mannerism, and not in itself fatal to great achievement or high inner worth.

Perhaps it means that America may yet do something worth while in the life of the spirit and the arts, without adopting the mores of the Left Bank. Human nature is so strange, don't you think?

IX

THE EMPEROR'S OLD CLOTHES

ONE day in the early 1840's a young Englishman named Martin Chuzzlewit, just arrived in this country for the purpose of making his fortune, was ushered into the office of the *New York Rowdy Journal* by its owner, Colonel Diver, and introduced to the editor, Mr. Jefferson Brick. The young Englishman was there at the invitation of Colonel Diver, who had boarded the transatlantic packet in quest of what we nowadays call ship news.

"You have heard of Jefferson Brick, sir," quoth the Colonel, with a smile. "England has heard of Jefferson Brick. Europe has heard of Jefferson Brick. Let me see. When did you leave England, sir?"

"Five weeks ago," said Martin.

"Five weeks ago," repeated the Colonel, thoughtfully. "Now let me ask you, sir, which of Mr. Brick's articles had become at that time the most obnoxious to the British Parliament and the Court of St. James's?"

When young Martin Chuzzlewit, with the native candor of the upper-class Englishman, ventured to doubt whether the British Parliament and the British Crown were in the habit of reading every word that Mr. Jefferson Brick wrote, his statement was received with amused incredulity. And in the course of the succeeding months, as young Chuzzlewit went back and forth in the United States, he found himself at every turn confronted with the two basic articles of what we should call to-day the American Credo: first, that young Queen Victoria, her ministers, and her lawmakers lived in permanent apprehension of American public opinion; and second, that this panic state in exalted British circles was amply justified by America's incomparably superior virtues. One of Martin's casual acquaintances in his Western travels is a certain Major Hannibal Chollop. The Major is a Worshiper of Freedom and testifies to his faith by the ready use of his pistol and his bowie knife. Concerning the Major as a typical American, the Honorable Elijah Pogram, member of Congress, has much to say:—

"Our fellow countryman is a model of a man, quite fresh from Natur's mould," said Pogram, with enthusiasm. "He is a true-born child of this free hemisphere. Verdant as the mountains of our country; flowing as our mineral Licks; unspiled by withering conventionalities as air our own broad and boundless Perearers! Rough he may be. So air our Barrs. Wild he may be.

So air our Buffalers. But he is a child of Natur' and a child of Freedom; and his boastful answer to the Despot and the Tyrant is that his bright home is in the Settin' Sun!"

Taking nothing for granted, I hereby hasten to state that my quotations are from a book called *Martin Chuzzlewit* by a man named Charles Dickens who paid his first visit to the United States in the year 1842. Now, very near this time a European writer of fairy tales named Hans Christian Andersen must have been at work on a story called "The Emperor's New Clothes," of which the plot is as follows: —

Two rogues appear at court and offer to weave for the Emperor a suit of clothes of such exquisitely rare texture as to be invisible to anybody who is a fool or who is unfit for the station he occupies. The pretenders are supplied with ample gold and silk thread which they stow away in their knapsacks, and spend the days sitting before empty looms and going through the motions of weaving. Court officials who are sent to report on the status of the Emperor's new clothes stare, grow uneasy, think fast, and come back to report progress. When the clothes are "finished" the Emperor himself goes in state to inspect, and only after the very slightest hesitation does he express his delight. Comes then the day when the Emperor walks in procession through the streets in his new clothes amid the admiration and acclaim of his people; until a little child calls out, "But the Emperor has nothing on!"

The Undressed Truth

Nobody, to my knowledge, has found it necessary to write a fable on human conduct entitled "The Emperor's Old Clothes." But that is probably because the need has already been met by the common adage about giving a dog a bad name. Just as you may take a naked man and persuade people to admire the beautiful clothes he is wearing, so you may take a man sufficiently and even respectably dressed and by exactly the same method of persuasion induce people to blush for his nakedness. You may go on being scandalized by the nudity of Jones until a little child breaks out crying because he cannot see the naked man that everybody is talking about. To the infant's eyes the man they are all pointing at seems to be decently equipped with coat, trousers, and shoes.

A brief parenthesis is necessary. When I say that people may be induced to see a naked man as magnificently arrayed and a decently dressed man as naked, I would seem to be contradicting the principal thesis of the present volume. Implied in every

chapter and specifically upheld in the chapter on
Propaganda is the contention that there are very
definite limits to what people may be persuaded
against the teachings of their basic, common, everyday experience; and it is basic experience to see a
naked man as naked and a covered man as dressed.
By what right do I now cite Hans Christian Andersen's satire on human gullibility and timidity for my
own special purposes?

Well, the answer is not difficult. It depends on
whom you mean by "people" in the original story.
It is obvious, is it not, that when Andersen makes a
little child assert the Emperor's nakedness, he means
something more than a child. He means the great
mass of simple people, who are not as susceptible as
their betters to current fads, fashions, formulas, discoveries, and revelations; they obstinately see what
they see and hear what they hear. But the Emperor and the court officials and the cheering crowds
that acquiesced in the invisible clothes were of the
better sort, were they not? They were the people
with whom this book is so largely concerned: the
people who cannot see Jones with the simple eyes
of Jones's immediate neighbors, but who see Jones
with eyes educated to the mode of the moment.
They will look upon a naked Jones and delight in
his beautiful invisible raiment, if the current hy-

pothesis demands it. They will look upon Jones in his familiar rough, serviceable tweeds and call him naked if the current philosophy has decided that Jones is naked — without putting the philosophers to the trouble of looking at Jones.

The latter thing is what happened to us in the decade of the 1920's. It was an era which concentrated passionately on the nakedness of Jones. It was an era which overlooked or forgot to mention or even went to the trouble of explaining away the garments which Jones did have on his body. To-day people are ready to admit that Jones after all was moderately well dressed all the time he was being held up to shame for his nakedness. The Rediscovery of Jones with which this series of chapters is concerned might have been called the Re-covering of Jones — the covering of his alleged nakedness with a set of garments which have all the time been there.

What are some of Jones's old clothes which a critical, satirical, revaluating decade succeeded in criticizing and revaluating out of existence? Let me reply in somewhat roundabout fashion by saying that a survey of the American scene to-day demands on the part of the observer a new mobilization of courage. In the period of insurgency just behind us it required no courage at all to say the most terrifying things about Jones. Everybody was doing it; that is to say, everybody who was anybody. That life in the United States was stale and cramped and stagnant, that freedom was a lie, that religion was a mask, that thought was the product of the hypodermic needle of Propaganda, that machines dominated a race of robots, that the human spark was extinct, that happiness was nonexistent, that love and laughter and dreams were infant phrases out of McGuffey's Reader — these things which at the beginning were regarded as challenging and devastating and Apocalyptic were in reality nothing of the kind. They became automatic, prescribed, *de rigueur*. You sat down to your typewriter and the nakedness of Jones clicked off on the blistering pages almost without the intervention of one's fingers.

A Hundred Years after Chuzzlewit

That trade practice is now fading. But we are still so near the years when a naked Jones dwelt in a miasmatic America that it requires a special mobilization of courage to affirm — to affirm — well, here goes, come what may — to affirm that at bottom Mr. Jefferson Brick and the Honorable Elijah Pogram were right; incomparably more in the right, at least, than the brick throwers and pogromists of the late unpleasantness. The present hour demands the courage to assert that the Fourth of July orator with his beetling brow and his unterrified cowlick and his right hand in the bosom of his black frock coat and his left hand raised to the Flag and the mammoth oral cavity emitting challenges to the Despots and the Tyrants and the Welkin and everybody else concerned or unconcerned — that this creature of comedy was — and is — in essence right. The hour calls for the courage to maintain that the historic American clichés — how much pain the thing which "cliché" describes has evoked in the ranks of the sensitive! — that the clichés, catchwords, stencils, "dope" of the Jefferson Bricks, the Elijah Pograms, the General Cyrus Chokes, had in them, and still have, the sturdy nucleus of truth.

Very nearly one hundred years after Jefferson Brick's articles caused shivers to run down the spine of Queen Victoria and her ministers, after Elijah Pogram saw the Tyrants and Despots of Europe go down 'neath the onward stride of the young Giant of the Settin' Sun, a French journalist addressed a meeting of American newspaper editors in Washington. The time was April 1930, and the speaker was the celebrated "Pertinax" of the *Écho de Paris*. And, among other things, this hard-boiled, tory French journalist said the following: —

The European problem cannot even be expressed in stable terms as long as the American unknown factor has not been replaced by a definite figure positive or negative. Your present position is unexampled in the history of the world.

You are supposed to be omnipotent, and recently you had only to take the trouble to file a request to get from proud England a 50 per cent share in the imperium of the seas. You have imposed on the whole of Europe the Covenant of the League of Nations — it was embodied in the Treaty of Versailles to suit the home politics of one of your residents, and, as a result, the whole development of post-war Europe was prejudiced.

Under your influence, the occupation of the Ruhr was scrapped, and the Dawes plan, to be followed by the Young plan, made a substitute for it. Only two years ago you intimated that you were willing to sign the Pact of Paris, and, as a consequence, the League's Covenant, your own creation of nine years before, was thrown back into the melting pot.

You are more than any other factor the cause of political Europe, as it stands to-day.

That the issue of the World War was decided by our intervention; that the future course of history in the Old World can be shaped in accordance with our own desires if only we see fit to make our desires known; that the basic problem of the future, world peace or world war, is for us to determine;

that there is under way in Europe a mighty process described as Americanization — these things are commonplaces to-day. But they are commonplaces which prove that Jefferson Brick and Elijah Pogram had the correct understanding of their country's destiny, whereas Charles Dickens erred in laying too much emphasis on the rôle of the Cuspidor in American civilization of his day.

That exaggerated emphasis on the spittoon we have witnessed in our own day, and for a whole decade.

What our querulous but veracious M. André Geraud ("Pertinax") has been saying about the rôle of America in the new world countless other observers have been saying: the Siegfrieds, the Maurois, the Bernard Faÿs, the Herriots, the Chestertons, the Bellocs, the Keyserlings, the Duhamels, the Wellses, the H. A. L. Fishers, the Ferreros, the Salveminis — it is a whole world of observers. A few of them speak even more sharply than "Pertinax." The majority of them speak in much more kindly fashion. Some of them are panicky about what we shall do to the rest of the world. More of them are equally glad and apprehensive. All of them are enormously impressed by this great reality of the present age — America already the strongest nation on earth and engaged in showing the way to the rest of the world. This is not Elijah Pogram speaking; it is the commonplace of the foreign observers. The great topic of to-day is America's world leadership, whether that leadership is to be for the world's good or ill.

Change of Intellectual Climate

The only people who in this decade remained unaware of great American destinies in the making were our own self-styled "articulate" classes. They were too busy elsewhere. They were so busy being articulate about the dreadful outrage perpetrated by the D.A.R. of West Brookfield in refusing to listen to a speaker of whom the Daughters disapproved that they had no time to notice China and India citing the American Declaration of Independence and the words of Abraham Lincoln. Our articulate classes were so exercised by the Boston censor that they had no time to ask themselves why the peoples of Europe were so eager to Americanize themselves. They were so exercised about the intellectual palsy of South Fork, Iowa (settled in 1890), and the spirit of regimentation in Ojibway College (founded in 1910), that they could not take note of an ancient foreign world which did not make epigrams about our small towns and our colleges, but which studied them seriously for the secret of that new life which seems destined to encompass the globe.

That indifference of American articulates to the essence of America is passing. I have exaggerated in saying that it requires special courage now to affirm the old American clichés. The thing is nowhere near so hazardous now as it would have been two years ago. Perhaps it is not hazardous at all, though obviously it still comes awkward to recite the old American catechism. It is awkward at the moment that I am writing these lines; but who knows? By the time they get into print the constraint may have worn off; we do move so fast in this country. In the most unexpected quarters, in the erstwhile citadels of challenge and revolution and devastation, voices are being raised to suggest that perhaps in this respect and in that respect we did not quite do justice to the United States. In a little while these tentative, exploratory apologies may have swelled to full choruses of praise. Men, upstanding and unashamed, may be speaking out loudly about America the land of opportunity, where a blacksmith's son may become President of the United States; America the land of asylum for millions of European refugees (until the other day), where an immigrant's son may make a splendid run for President of the United States on the Democratic ticket; America the land of equality, which knows no caste or class, but where everyone is a son of freedom and a foe to tyrants — though voting, of course, the straight party ticket. Yes, it is far from inconceivable that in this febrile America, with its genius for doing things up brown, we may soon have everybody telling everybody else — in the papers and the magazines and the novels and the plays — that Jefferson Brick and Elijah Pogram were right.

This may come soon; yet undeniably, as I read over these lines in my visible typewriter in the spring of 1931 they sound raucous. They exaggerate dreadfully. They overstate the case against the deflaters of the 1920's even as these overstated the case against their inflated predecessors. But what is to be done about it? It used to be said, quite justly, that belligerents in the course of hostilities tend to become like each other — on the unpleasant side. They borrow each other's less desirable characteristics. That is now happening in present chapter and book. Well, perhaps it is in the eternal justice of things that in defending Democracy one should be almost as unfair to the Baltimore Superman as he was in his time to the facts of Democracy. In stating the case of Jones against the Civilized Minority it is far from unpleasant to tip the scale a bit against the

Civilized Minority, as it used to work the trick against Jones.

Of the members of this Civilized Minority it may justly be said — and as a matter of fact it has been said again and again in the course of these pages — that they were so passionately interested in being a minority that they had no time to be interested in the facts of civilization. What interested them was the epigrams and the phrases and the Heaven-sent but unproven theories about civilization. What interested them was the exceptions — the irritating exceptions of life that mean so much more to a sensitive minority than the rules of life.

Take for instance, and at somewhat greater length, this Americanization of Europe to which I alluded a little while ago. In reply to my little hymn of glory about the rôle of America among the nations, the Minoritarian may reply quite effectively — at first sight — with a comprehensive "What of it?" Suppose America does come to rule the world? What satisfaction is there in thinking of America as powerful enough to impose upon the rest of the world her tooth pastes and her chewing gum and her ice-cream soda and her bathtubs and even her radios and her automobiles? It only means that America's pernicious gold-dust twins, Babbitt and the Puritan, whose strangle hold on free emotion and free intelligence we have been striving to break in our own country, are now imposing themselves on the rest of the world. The world is being Americanized. What of it?

A New Line of Americana

Well, the reply to the Minoritarian comes in two clauses:—

1. The fact that the world is being Americanized is in itself a phenomenon that deserves the respectful attention of one interested, like yourself, in Civilization. It has been your contention that America is beset by plagues peculiarly her own. In your assault upon Puritanism and materialism in the United States you have implied — indeed, you have openly charged — that elsewhere men are happily free of such infections. You have drawn up lists of inanities and tyrannies and labeled them "Americana." But now it appears that these lists of Americana are being bought in ever greater quantities by the other nations for textbook use. Does n't it seem reasonable, in the face of a world going American, to ask you to look over your original notes and arguments on America to see whether you may not have slipped up here and there? It may be fairly easy to indict a whole nation. It is not so easy to indict a whole world. It is permissible to suggest that it may not

be a case of everybody being out of step except your boy Mike.

2. But the weightier clause in the rejoinder has to do with the essence of this Americanization process now at work among the peoples. The Civilized Minoritarian refuses to take comfort in the thought that soon the whole world will be drinking American chocolate sodas, dancing to jazz, gleaming with golden dentistry, and running about in automobiles. To this summary of Americanization most of us subscribe and in so doing we miss the heart of the matter.

We speak of Americanization in terms of ice cream, jazz, and radios. We forget the Americanization of higher wages which underlies these material gains, but which carries a social-spiritual gain greater than these gains. We forget the Americanization of equality and opportunity. We forget that the rise of the European masses to a higher standard of living has been paralleled by the rise of the masses to a fuller rôle in life of the nations. The real Americanization of Germany in recent years is to be seen in Socialist Chancellors presiding over German cabinets. The real Americanization of England is the British Labor Party in power and in fruitful activity.

We speak of the Americanization of the Far East

and picture a Shanghai student in American clothes or a Bombay student shouting into an American megaphone. But it is the real Americanization when our Shanghai student parades the streets with a thousand other students demanding freedom of the press, free elections, universal suffrage. We overlook the real thing in Americanization when the Bombay broadcaster summons the masses of India to a government based on full equality of race, creed, class; and, in support of that ideal, quotes from Thomas Jefferson and Abraham Lincoln.

We see the Americanization of Europe in terms of American bars and tiled bathrooms. But we overlook the Americanization of Europe in terms of high schools and colleges for the people. The advanced nations of Europe have primary schools just as good as ours, and in the matter of popular literacy they are better off than we are. The primary schools of Europe have been the People's Schools; beyond the primary school it was not thought desirable or possible to carry the people. But the United States has 5,000,000 boys and girls in the high schools as against 750,000 children in the German secondary schools and 600,000 children in the British secondary schools. In proportion to the population we have nearly four times as many children in the high schools as Germany; three times as many as Great

Britain. Yet for Germany the figures to-day already register her Americanization since the war; her 750,000 children in the secondary schools are an increase of 50 per cent over the year 1911, with the same population. Great Britain before the war had 250,000 children in the secondary schools. She now has, as we have seen, more than twice as many, for the same population as before the war.

They Go to School

Our social observers have been so busy with the phenomena of American repression in West Brookfield and Seattle that they have failed to take note of the American high school. A great British authority on education, Sir Michael Sadler, has called the high school the most important single contribution to modern social life. And I trust the reader will bear with me if I cite at some length testimony from the Germany of after the war. It is testimony which is sufficiently important in its specific application, but more so because of the horizons it opens up. My quotation is from an article by Professor Carl H. Becker of the University of Berlin, and Prussian Minister of Education from 1919 to 1930, in *School and Society* for November 22, 1930: —

The educational policy of the old days set up a dual system. One part of this system embraced the secondary schools, the technical colleges and the universities. The other embraced the *Volksschule* (People's Schools) or elementary schools. The difference between these two was something more than a difference in the grade of teaching; it was rather a difference between the respective functions which the two sections discharged. Those who attended the elementary schools were shut out from the higher schools and colleges. The former catered to one class of the population and the latter to another. In our social life these two classes never mingled with one another. It was much the same as in the military organization, where the chasm that separated the officer class from the common soldiers was impassable. Only in rare cases could those who had graduated from our elementary schools proceed to the higher grades of education in the secondary schools and universities.

The division of our people into two cultural groups, which developed apart from each other and finally came to a stage where it was impossible for the one to understand the other, has been explicitly and almost wholly set aside under the new régime. Not that everybody must now attend the higher schools and the universities. In the very nature of things that would be unthinkable; and, from the economic point of view, it would be only a wild dream. Nor has the new state decreed that all the children of men are born with like natures and like talents, and that they ought to be given equal opportunities to develop them accordingly. So long as humanity is made up of men and women, and not of machines that may be ordered from some factory or other, so long will we have to deal with personal aptitudes of various kinds, demanding a corresponding variety in our system of teaching.

The chief difference, from this point of view, between the educational policy of the old régime and that of nowadays is that diversity of talent is recognized as a dispensation of nature, and that the student who gives evidence of high-class mental powers must be given a chance to develop them, no matter to what social group he may belong. In other words, the facilities for higher education are no longer the privilege of the wealthier or the aristocratic classes of the community.

And you will be pleased to learn, from the account which I intend to give you, that American educational ideals have stood as sponsors for this reform.

Here is an Americanization of Europe never hinted at in the dirges about American tooth paste and radios in the citadels of ancient European culture. Europe is now Americanizing itself from one university student for every 700 of the population in Germany and in Great Britain to one college or university student for every 125 of the population in the United States.

And again the Minoritarian will say, "What of it?" Suppose Europe in the matter of educational anarchy does sink to our own level. Suppose Babbitt and Bluenose flourish in the British universities, and mediocrity triumphs in the German gymnasia, and the drag upon first-class minds becomes as heavy in Europe as it is in America; what then? Do you expect me to get up and sing about it?

But that, of course, is quibble. The invasion of the high schools and the universities by the masses may do all these dreadful things to European education and culture. The fact remains that our Minoritarian would never handle American ideals on education as cavalierly as he has done if he had noted that the rest of the world is swinging to the American ideal. For the moment we are not concerned with the results of the educational revolution in the Old World; the fact in itself is significant. And if there is anything upon which the Critical Intelligence in the United States has prided itself, it is the capacity, the positive relish for Facing Facts Fearlessly. Let it, then, face the fact that Elijah Pogram was right when he thrust his right hand into the bosom of his frock coat and saluted the little red schoolhouse. The march of history has vindicated Elijah. The great issue before the nations to-day, certainly next after the organization of world peace, possibly ahead of it, is elementary schools for the masses of India and China, more high schools and colleges for the plain people of Great Britain and Germany.

Will it be at the ultimate cost of Civilization? Possibly. But the experiment is bound to be made. It is inevitable; and the Critical Intelligence is proud of its courage in facing the inevitable. Whether we of the Better Sort like it or not, the experiment is bound to get itself tried out all over the world — the experiment which began in this country, and men called it Democracy.

The Lure of Cæsar

The vindication of Jones against the charge of nudity is not out of place, I think, in a study dealing with the rediscovery of the facts about Jones. I have tried to show that the American Jones is not walking about in a state of indecent exposure. He is still wearing his suit of old democratic clothes, and with a degree of comfort that is attracting the attention of his European and Asiatic neighbors. To restate the simple facts of American democracy as against the misrepresentations of the embittered and the disillusioned is to serve the objective truth.

But there is to-day a reason warmer and more compelling than Objective Truth to make Americans look at their democracy, and, without blinking its faults, to rejoice in its powers, its virtues, and its promise. One may go further. In the interest of the higher good, much will be forgiven Jones if for a little while he closes his eyes to the minor faults in his democracy in order to preserve his basic faith in the Democratic Experiment as a whole. This is excusable because it is evident that plain Mr. Jones for some time to come will have to maintain the defense of his democratic institutions against a new outbreak of the Critical Temper. That temper has found a fascinating new formula to play with. It is called Cæsarism, and its purpose is to have a good time with the lives and destinies of multitudes of simple men.

When I said some time back that our articulate classes, what with the Boston censor and the West Brookfield D.A.R. and the editor of the *Osawatomie Clarion,* were too busy to take note of the really important things going on in the world, I was guilty of overstatement. Our articulate classes did take note of world developments. They noted the appearance in the post-Armistice world of the Dictatorship idea; and many of them hastened to succumb to the white dictatorship of Fascism and the red dictatorship of Communism with that swooning abandon which always seizes upon the peculiarly sensitive mind in the presence of a bright new formula.

The breakdown of Democracy; the bankruptcy of representative institutions and the Parliamentary system; the demonstrated inefficiency of our economic system of private enterprise; our absurdly quaint notions about personal and civil liberty; our Government by Palaver; the magnificent purposiveness of Signor Mussolini; the superb axe-strokes of the Soviet method; the new Will to Achieve (White or Red), as against our old will just to keep things going and everybody have a good time; the Clean Slate, as the Bolshevists have cleaned the Russian slate, against our system of patchwork compromise — the spell of these new formulas and experiments has been strong upon observers and thinkers. The itch to gamble with the lives and destinies of common men, to make men richer, better, more efficient by violence, that itch is still in the flesh of some of our intellectuals, that fever is still in their blood.

Consider the amazing record set by Fascism in the matter of sanitary arrangements on the Italian railroads! (American democrats notoriously do not clean their railroad coaches.) Ponder the astounding results of the Proletarian Dictatorship in the matter of hiring American engineers to build factories in Russia. (American engineers never build factories at home.) Consider these fascinating Experiments! (You begin by calling them experiments; but in the heat of the argument you forget that the things are supposed to be experiments and you salute them as demonstrations; looking at which, we are invited to say whether the time has not come for junking this antiquated Democracy of ours.)

And liberty? And the right of a man to have a say in his fate? And other features of our own Democratic Experiment, which creaks, no doubt, which does not hit on all sixteen cylinders, which comes high to operate, but which has kept us happy and which is now being imitated in Europe and in Asia? The Experimenter lifts his brows: My dear fellow, Liberty! Such an old-fashioned note to strike in the year 1931! And he has no difficulty in showing you that Liberty really became obsolete in the year 1911 when somebody invented a gadget attachable to a whoozis and so initiated something Dynamic and Technological as a result of which our former ideas of liberty based on nineteenth-century economics went to the scrap heap.

And human happiness? And human worth? And the right of a man to be a man, and not a wheel in the mighty mechanism of the Fascist State, or a chunk of fuel in the blazing furnace of the Soviet State? The right of a man to be a man instead of cannon fodder for a State or raw material for an Economic System?

Up go the eyebrows again. My dear fellow! My dear, dear Jones! Don't you know that you are not really ever a free agent or a man under your own

vaunted Democracy? Don't you know that in economics you are the slave of your employer, who
makes you live and feel and think as he pleases?
Don't you know that politically you are the plaything of your Boss, who deludes you and bamboozles
you and buys your vote and makes you do what he
likes? Don't you know that as a plain average man
you are not free? And, what is more, you don't want
to be free and are not fit to be free? You want someone to think for you and decide for you and grow
angry for you and feel glad for you. Don't you
know . . . My dear fellow! My dear, dear Jones!

Under the circumstances, what is Jones to do?

One thing that Jones may do is to look the other
man in the face and say, as common men have been
known to say under provocation, "That is a lie.
I know I am a free man and I feel like a free man.
And the reason you want me to give up my freedom
and become a Fascist cog or a Communist commodity is that you have got hold of a bright new
formula and you want to try it out on me. Here's
your hat. The exit is on the left."

Well, now, what could I have been thinking of!
I must have been under the impression that this was
a conversation between an Anti–Humanist and a
Humanist, and not a conversation between Jones
and one of his Betters. For if Jones will occasionally

resort to strong language with his equals, he is never disrespectful to his Betters. Jones, I believe on second thought, will say nothing offensive to the man who has just asked him how he would like to move out of his rowdy, noisy, uncoördinated house of Democracy, and go to live in that admirably planned, built, and supervised apartment advertised by the Red and White Cæsars for the very reasonable rent of your body and soul. Jones, with his American diffidence in the presence of learning, his American good nature and open-mindedness, will say that he will be glad to look into the matter and as soon as he has come to a decision, why, he will give the Experimenter a buzz.

But that is as far as it will go. For Jones, without sitting down to ponder the problem, will know, with all the resources of that basic wisdom which his Betters have denied him, that this shining new formula of the Efficient Dictator is a deadly menace to him, Jones the common man, and to the stock of human dignity and worth and prestige that he has built up in the generations of our own Democratic Experiment. Knowing all that, Jones will probably go out and cast his ballot as part of the local Irish vote, or Jewish vote, or German vote, or Native American vote, or Italian, or anti-Catholic vote . . .

Well, what of it? Some day, we hope and trust,

America will be rid of her Native American vote, her German, Jewish, Italian, Irish, anti-Catholic and pro-Protestant votes. But it is infinitely better that these separatist loyalties and prejudices continue to assert themselves than that they be abolished by the simple expedient of abolishing the manhood and the human status of the men who cherish them. Colonel Diver published the *Rowdy Journal* — well, rowdy, but human; and not the sub-humanity of the new Red and White Formulas.